MAX AXIOM AND THE SOCIETY OF SUPER SCIENTISTS

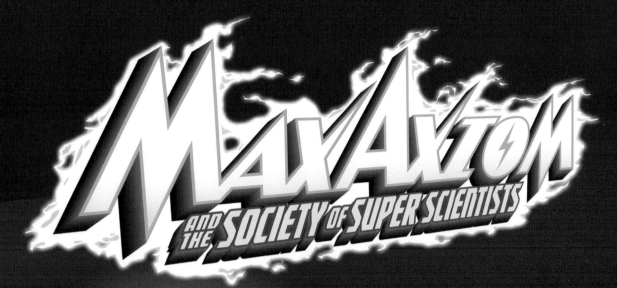

RAIN FOREST DESTRUCTION

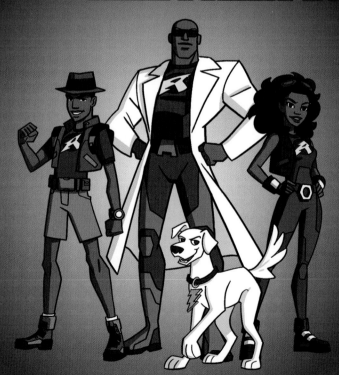

WRITTEN BY CAROL KIM
ILLUSTRATED BY EDUARDO GARCIA
COVER BY ERIK DOESCHER

CAPSTONE PRESS
a capstone imprint

Published by Capstone Press, an imprint of Capstone.
1710 Roe Crest Drive
North Mankato, Minnesota 56003
capstonepub.com

Library of Congress Cataloging-in-Publication Data
Names: Kim, Carol, author. | Garcia, Eduardo, 1970 August 31– illustrator.
Title: Rain forest destruction : a Max Axiom super scientist adventure /
    by Carol Kim ; illustrated by Eduardo Garcia.
Description: North Mankato, Minnesota : Capstone Press, [2022] |
    Series: Max Axiom and the society of super scientists | Includes
    bibliographical references and index. | Audience: Ages 8–11 |
    Audience: Grades 4–6
Identifiers: LCCN 2021012676 (print) | LCCN 2021012677 (ebook) |
    ISBN 9781663907554 (hardcover) | ISBN 9781663921772 (paperback) |
    ISBN 9781663907523 (ebook PDF) | ISBN 9781663907547 (kindle edition)
Subjects: LCSH: Deforestation—Juvenile literature. | Rain forest
    conservation—Juvenile literature. | Rain forest conservation—Comic
    books, strips, etc.
Classification: LCC SD418 .K56 2022 (print) | LCC SD418 (ebook) |
    DDC 333.75/16—dc23
LC record available at https://lccn.loc.gov/2021012676
LC ebook record available at https://lccn.loc.gov/2021012677

Summary: Trees are being cut down around the world. But why are rain
forests being cleared, and what happens if they disappear? Max Axiom
and the Society of Super Scientists are on a mission to find out! Go on
an exciting, fact-filled adventure to learn about the causes and effects of
deforestation and discover steps we can all take to protect these fragile
ecosystems.

Editorial Credits
Editors: Abby Huff and Aaron Sautter; Designer: Brann Garvey; Media
Researcher: Svetlana Zhurkin; Production Specialist: Kathy McColley

Cover Art by Erik Doescher

All internet sites appearing in back matter were available and accurate
when this book was sent to press.

Printed and bound in the United States of America. PO4270

TABLE OF CONTENTS

THE SOCIETY OF SUPER SCIENTISTS

MAX AXIOM

After years of study, Max Axiom, the world's first Super Scientist, knew the mysteries of the universe were too vast for one person alone to uncover. So Max created the Society of Super Scientists! Using their superpowers and super-smarts, this talented group investigates today's most urgent scientific and environmental issues and learns about actions everyone can take to solve them.

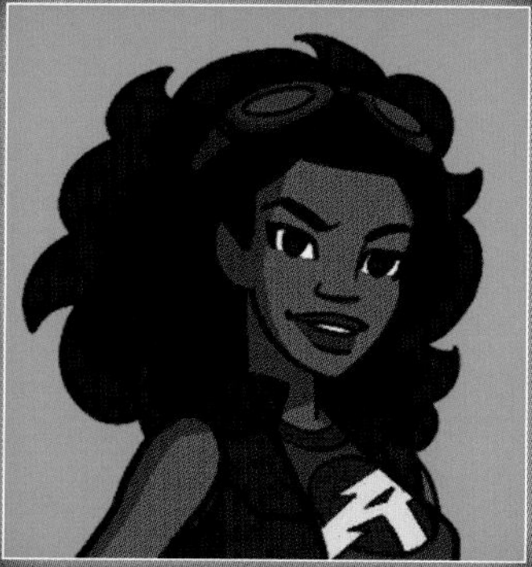

LIZZY AXIOM

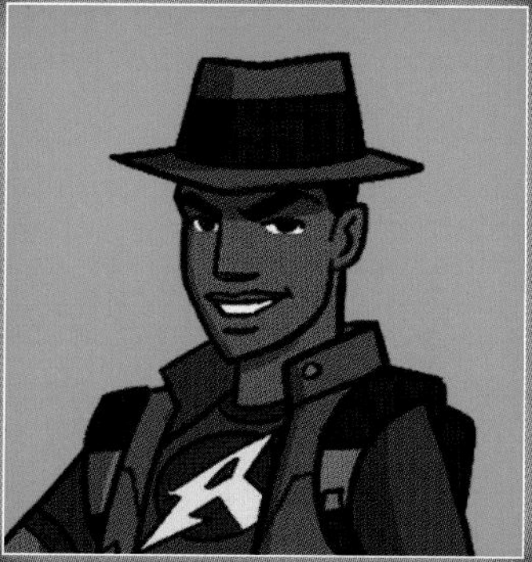

NICK AXIOM

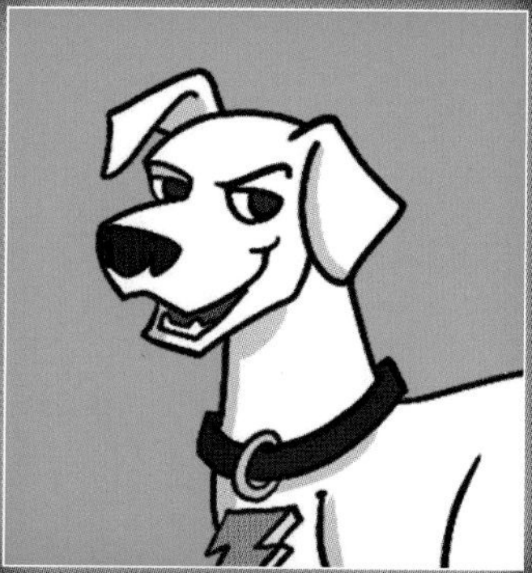

SPARK

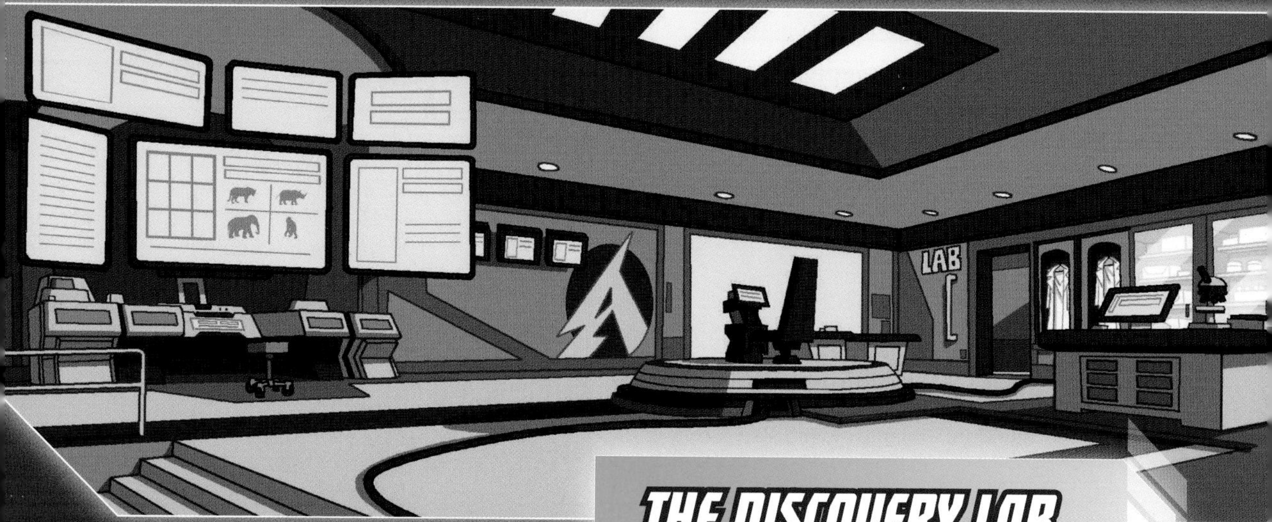
LAB

THE DISCOVERY LAB

Home of the Society of Super Scientists, this state-of-the-art lab houses advanced tools for cutting-edge research and radical scientific innovation. More importantly, it is a space for Super Scientists to collaborate and share knowledge as they work together to tackle any challenge.

SECTION 1: UNDER THREAT

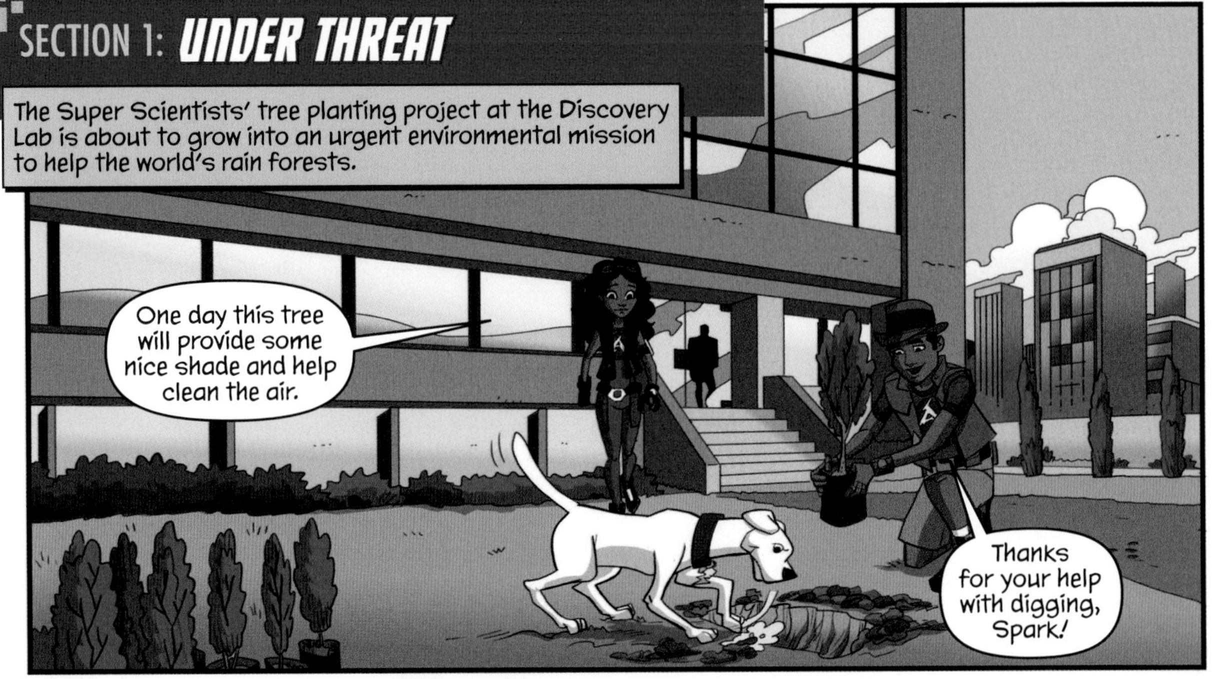
The Super Scientists' tree planting project at the Discovery Lab is about to grow into an urgent environmental mission to help the world's rain forests.
One day this tree will provide some nice shade and help clean the air.
Thanks for your help with digging, Spark!

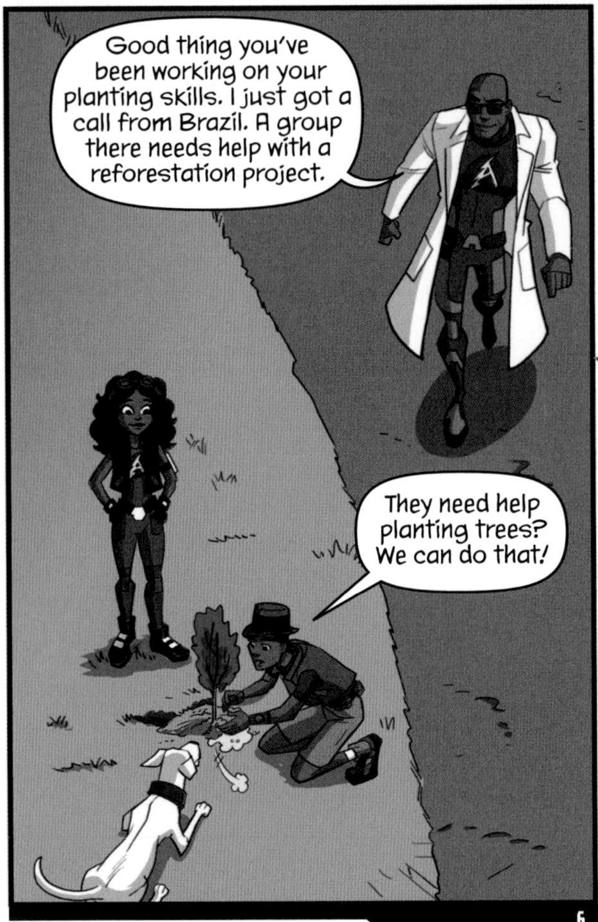
Good thing you've been working on your planting skills. I just got a call from Brazil. A group there needs help with a reforestation project.
They need help planting trees? We can do that!

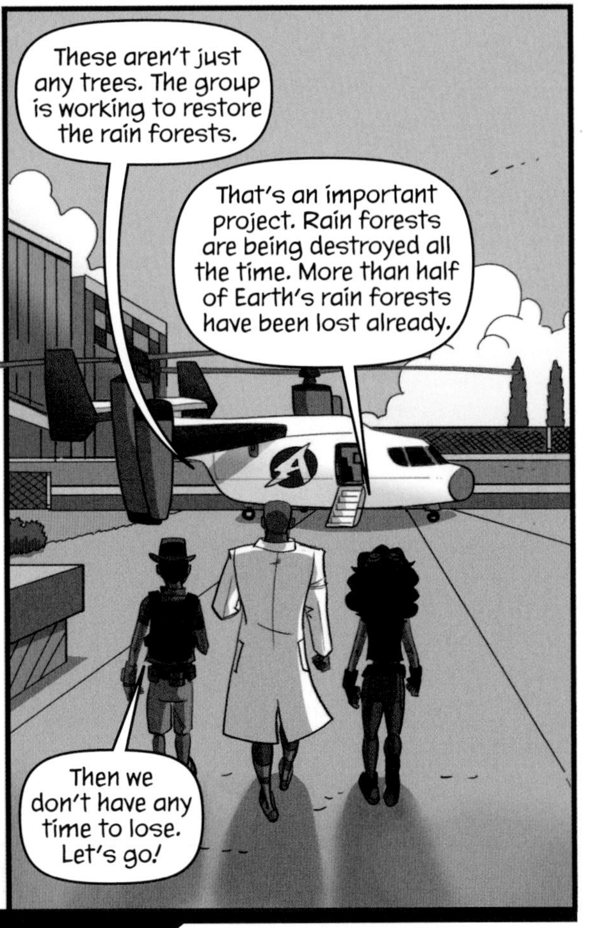
These aren't just any trees. The group is working to restore the rain forests.
That's an important project. Rain forests are being destroyed all the time. More than half of Earth's rain forests have been lost already.
Then we don't have any time to lose. Let's go!

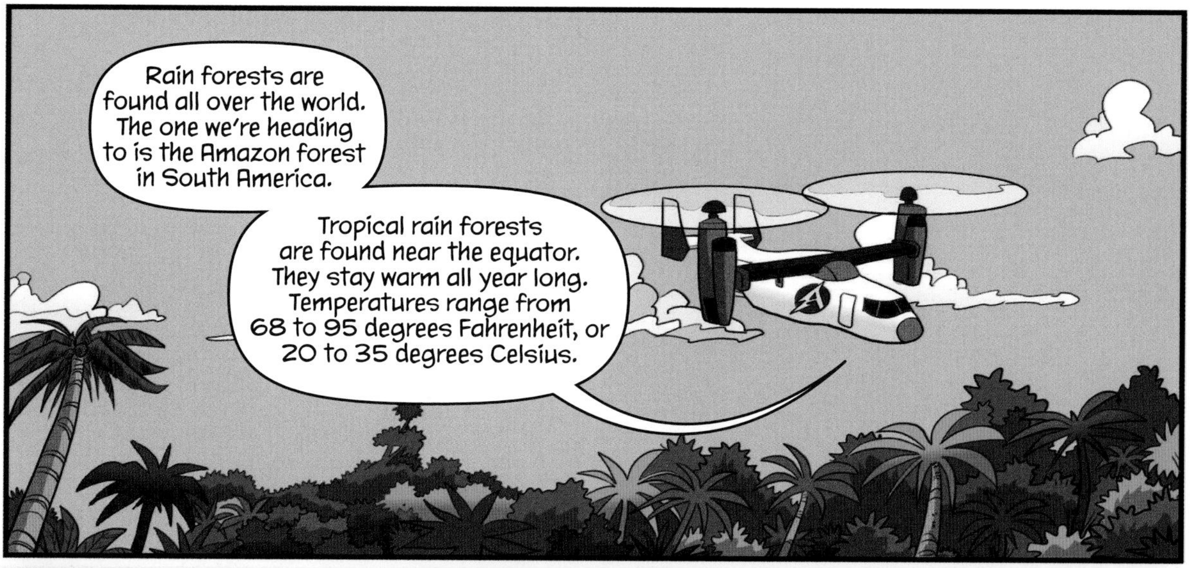
Rain forests are found all over the world. The one we're heading to is the Amazon forest in South America.
Tropical rain forests are found near the equator. They stay warm all year long. Temperatures range from 68 to 95 degrees Fahrenheit, or 20 to 35 degrees Celsius.

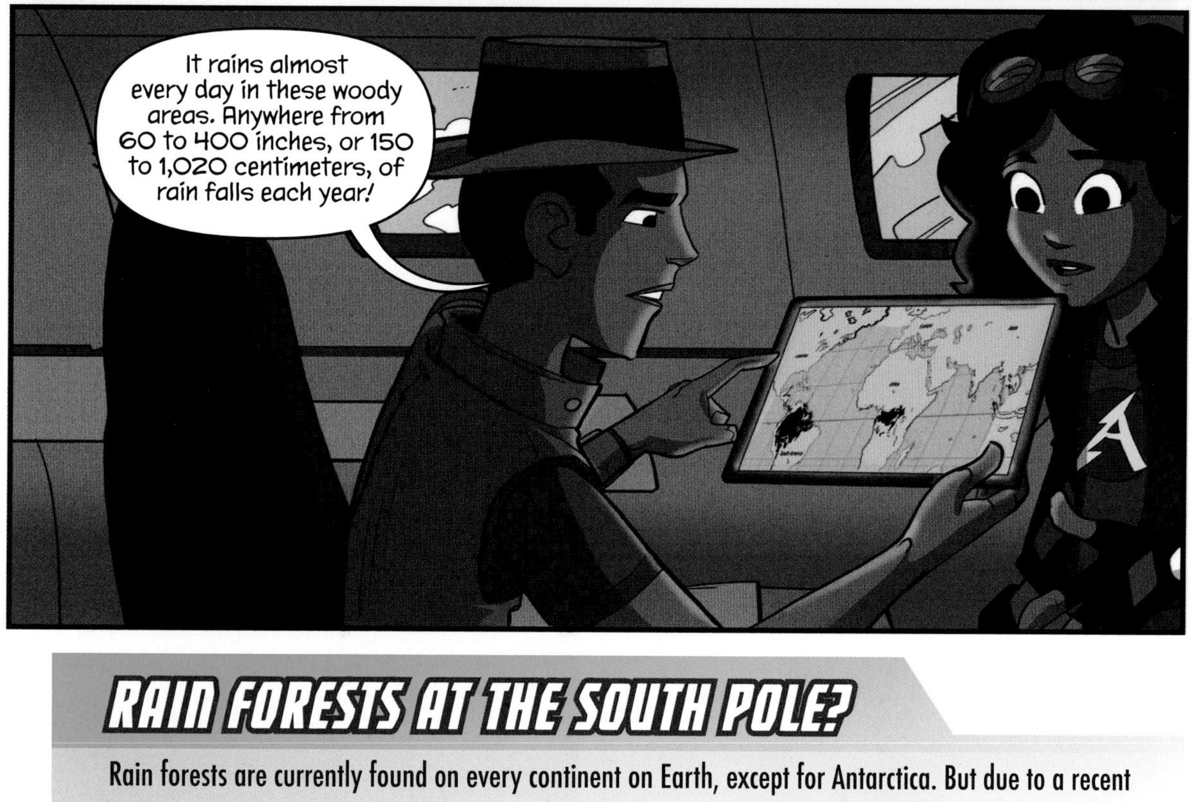
It rains almost every day in these woody areas. Anywhere from 60 to 400 inches, or 150 to 1,020 centimeters, of rain falls each year!

RAIN FORESTS AT THE SOUTH POLE?

Rain forests are currently found on every continent on Earth, except for Antarctica. But due to a recent discovery, the South Pole no longer has to be left out—at least if you count rain forests that existed 90 million years ago! Scientists drilling deep in the ground in West Antarctica discovered traces of an ancient forest. Plant remains in soil samples show the area was once home to a temperate rain forest, which has cooler temperatures than a tropical forest.

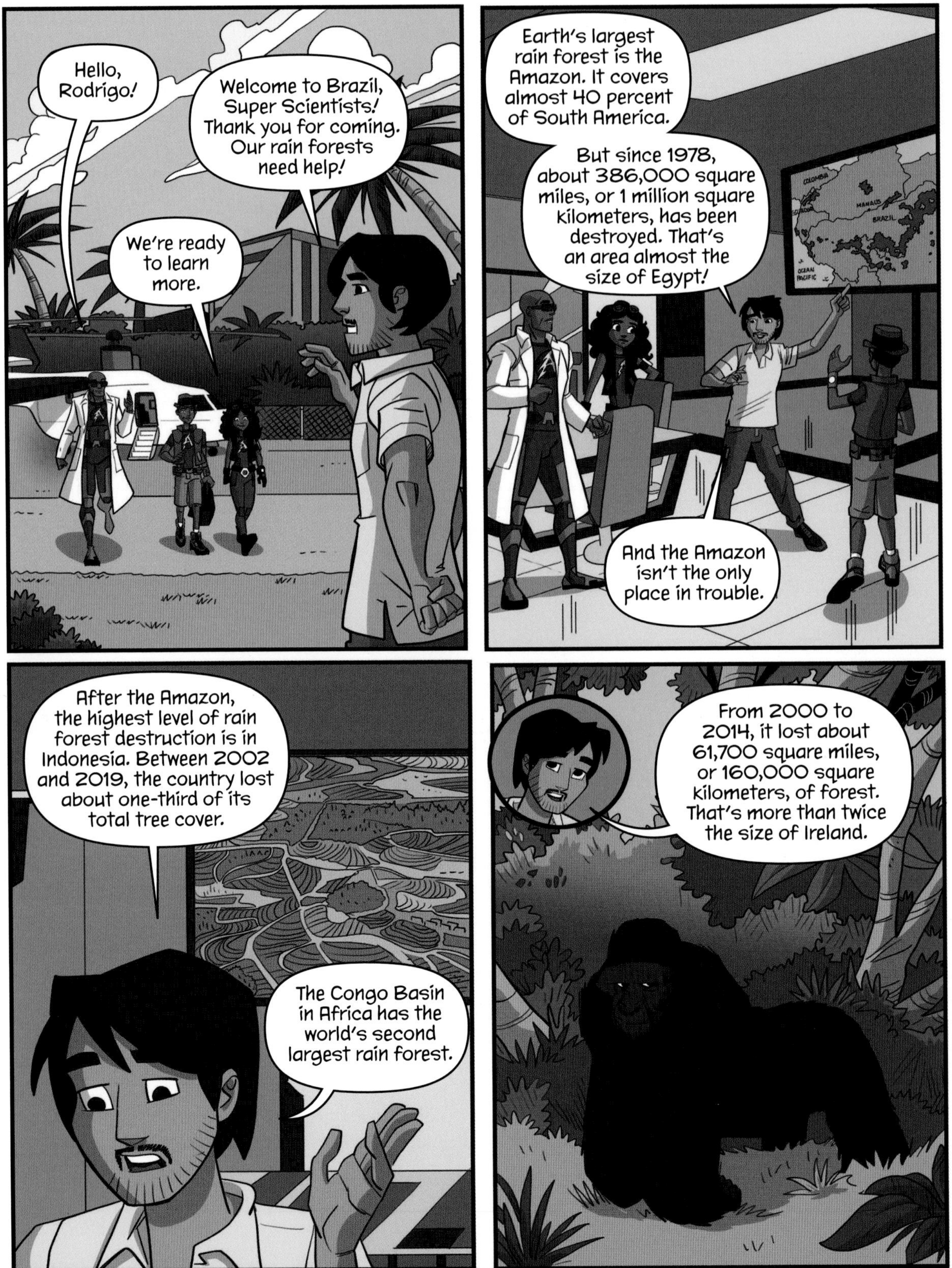

Hello, Rodrigo!
Welcome to Brazil, Super Scientists! Thank you for coming. Our rain forests need help!
We're ready to learn more.
Earth's largest rain forest is the Amazon. It covers almost 40 percent of South America.
But since 1978, about 386,000 square miles, or 1 million square kilometers, has been destroyed. That's an area almost the size of Egypt!
COLOMBIA
MANAUS
BRAZIL
OCEAN PACIFIC
And the Amazon isn't the only place in trouble.
After the Amazon, the highest level of rain forest destruction is in Indonesia. Between 2002 and 2019, the country lost about one-third of its total tree cover.
The Congo Basin in Africa has the world's second largest rain forest.
From 2000 to 2014, it lost about 61,700 square miles, or 160,000 square kilometers, of forest. That's more than twice the size of Ireland.

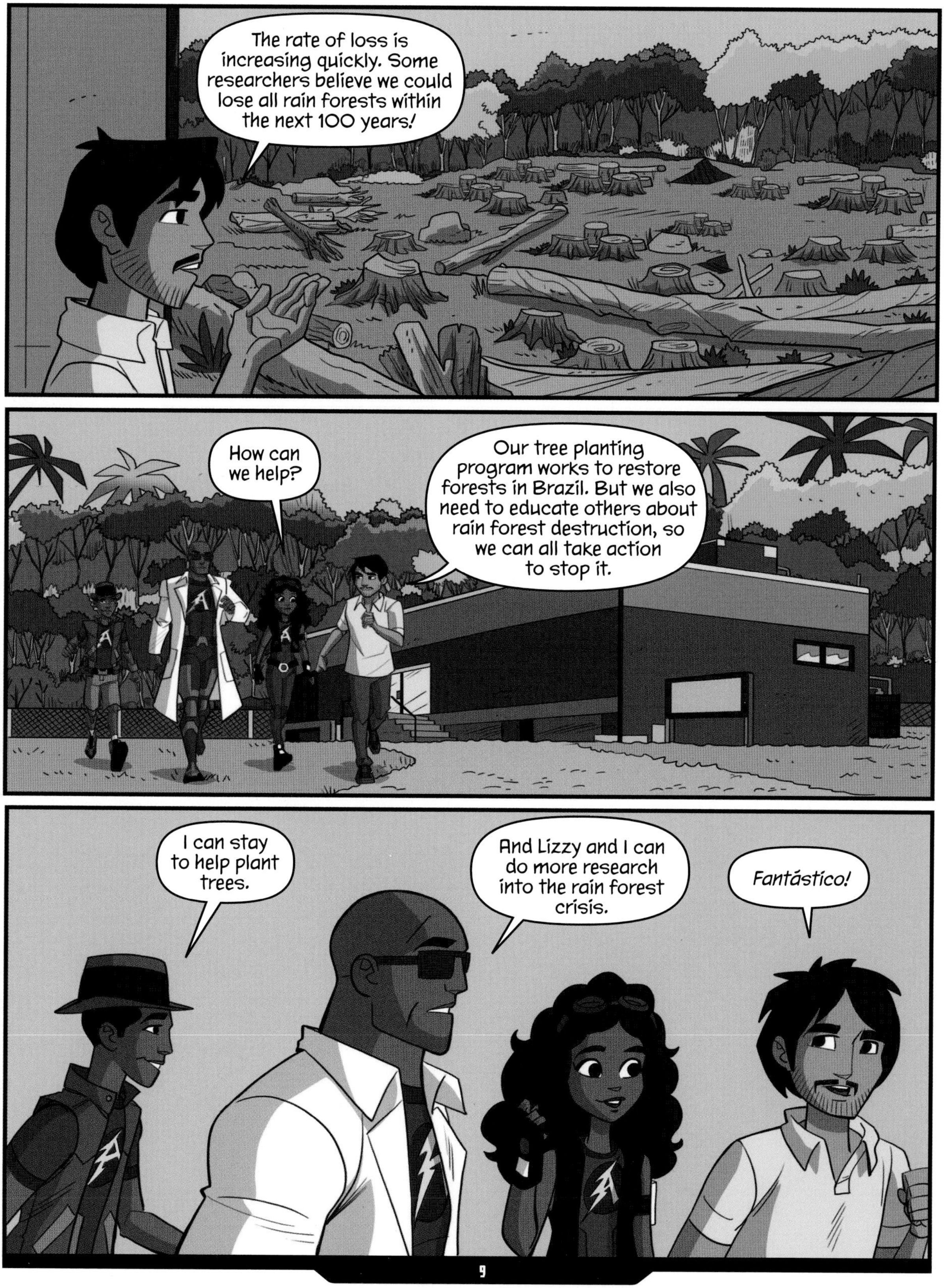
The rate of loss is increasing quickly. Some researchers believe we could lose all rain forests within the next 100 years!
How can we help?
Our tree planting program works to restore forests in Brazil. But we also need to educate others about rain forest destruction, so we can all take action to stop it.
I can stay to help plant trees.
And Lizzy and I can do more research into the rain forest crisis.
Fantástico!

SECTION 2: *BEHIND THE DESTRUCTION*

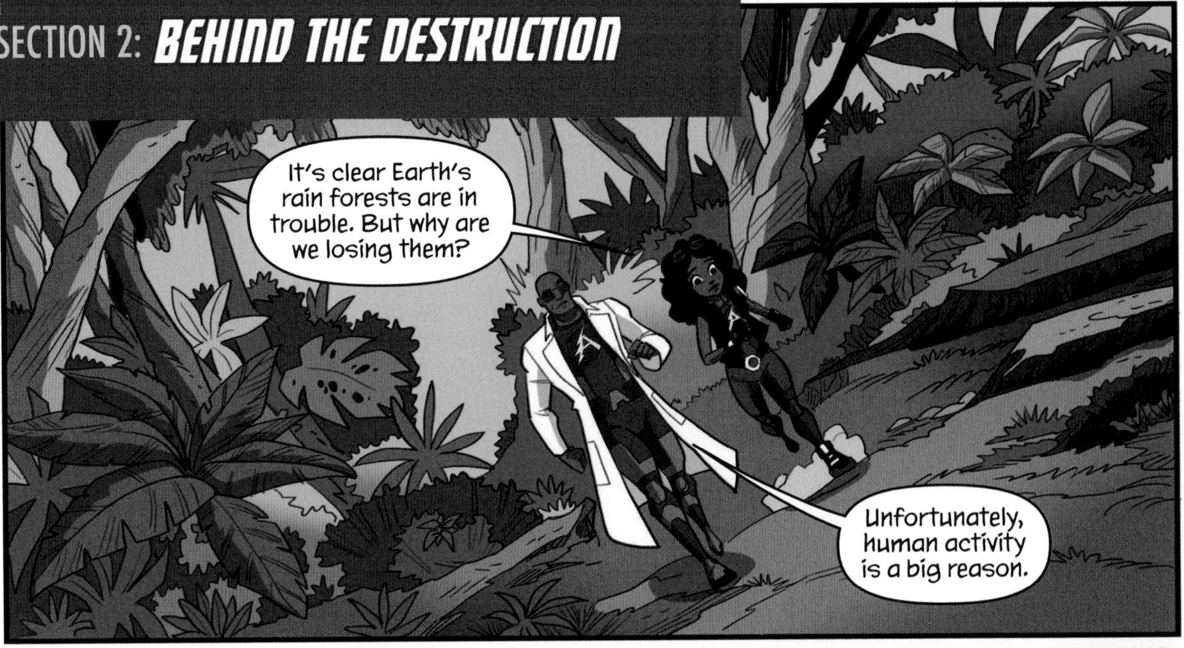
It's clear Earth's rain forests are in trouble. But why are we losing them?
Unfortunately, human activity is a big reason.

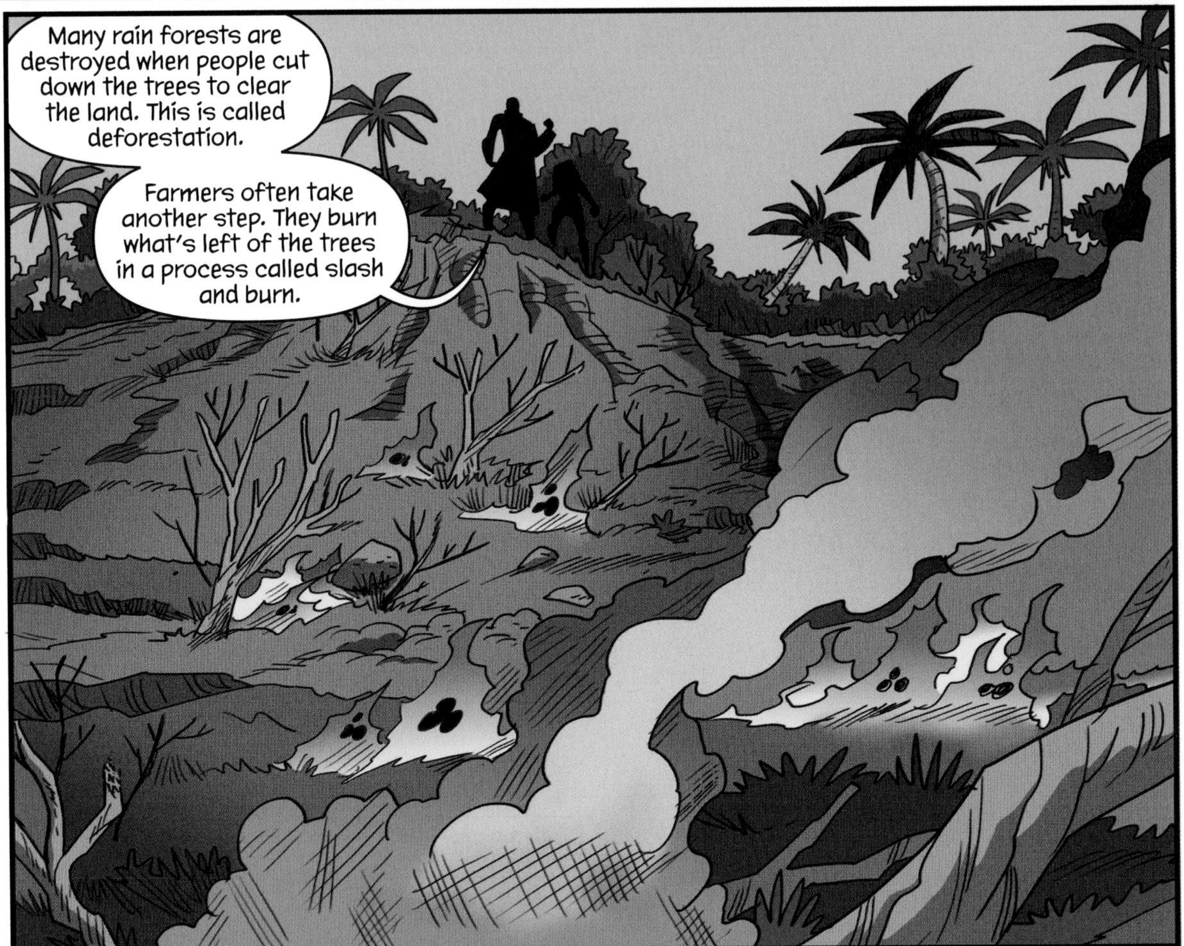
Many rain forests are destroyed when people cut down the trees to clear the land. This is called deforestation.
Farmers often take another step. They burn what's left of the trees in a process called slash and burn.

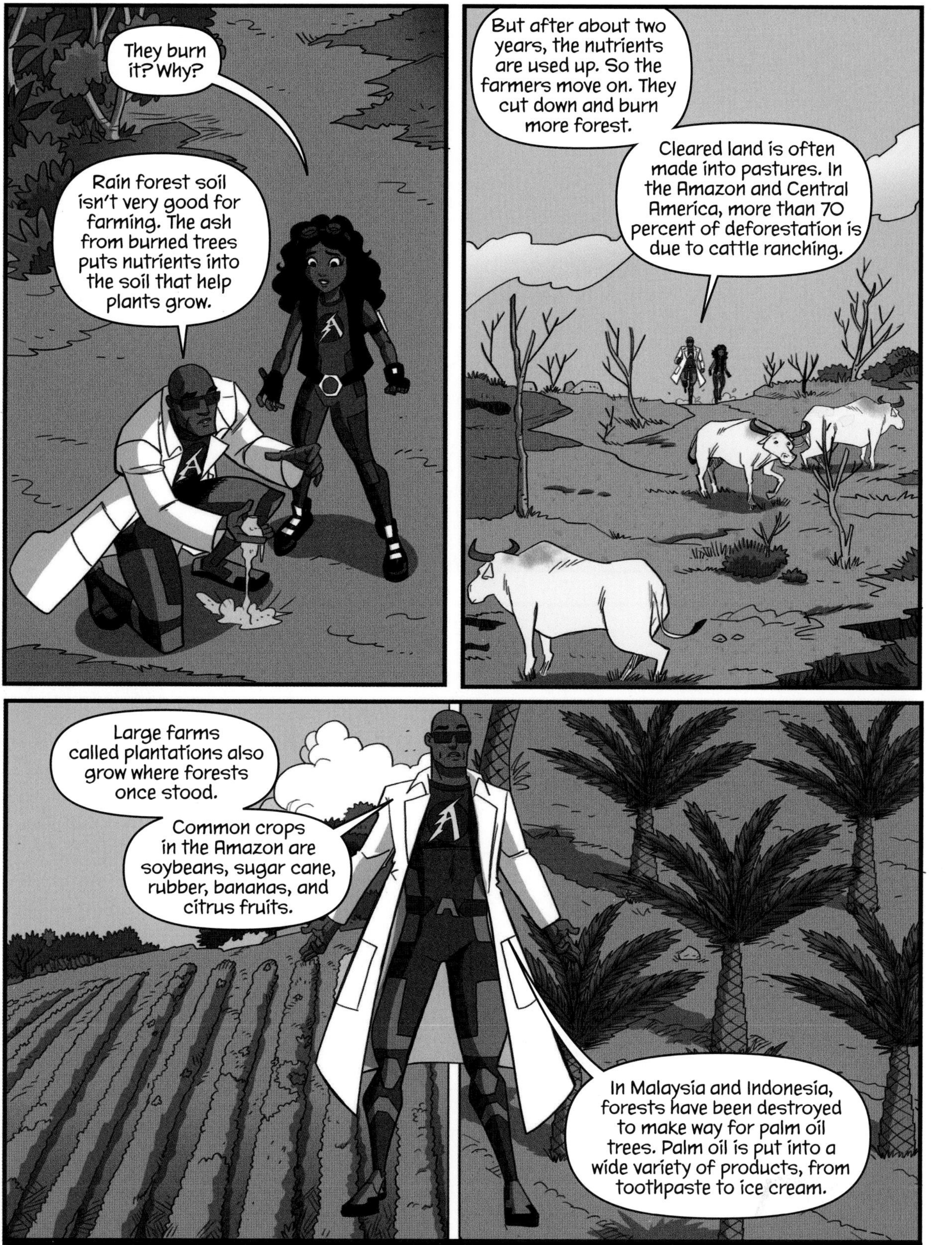
They burn it? Why?
Rain forest soil isn't very good for farming. The ash from burned trees puts nutrients into the soil that help plants grow.
But after about two years, the nutrients are used up. So the farmers move on. They cut down and burn more forest.
Cleared land is often made into pastures. In the Amazon and Central America, more than 70 percent of deforestation is due to cattle ranching.
Large farms called plantations also grow where forests once stood.
Common crops in the Amazon are soybeans, sugar cane, rubber, bananas, and citrus fruits.
In Malaysia and Indonesia, forests have been destroyed to make way for palm oil trees. Palm oil is put into a wide variety of products, from toothpaste to ice cream.

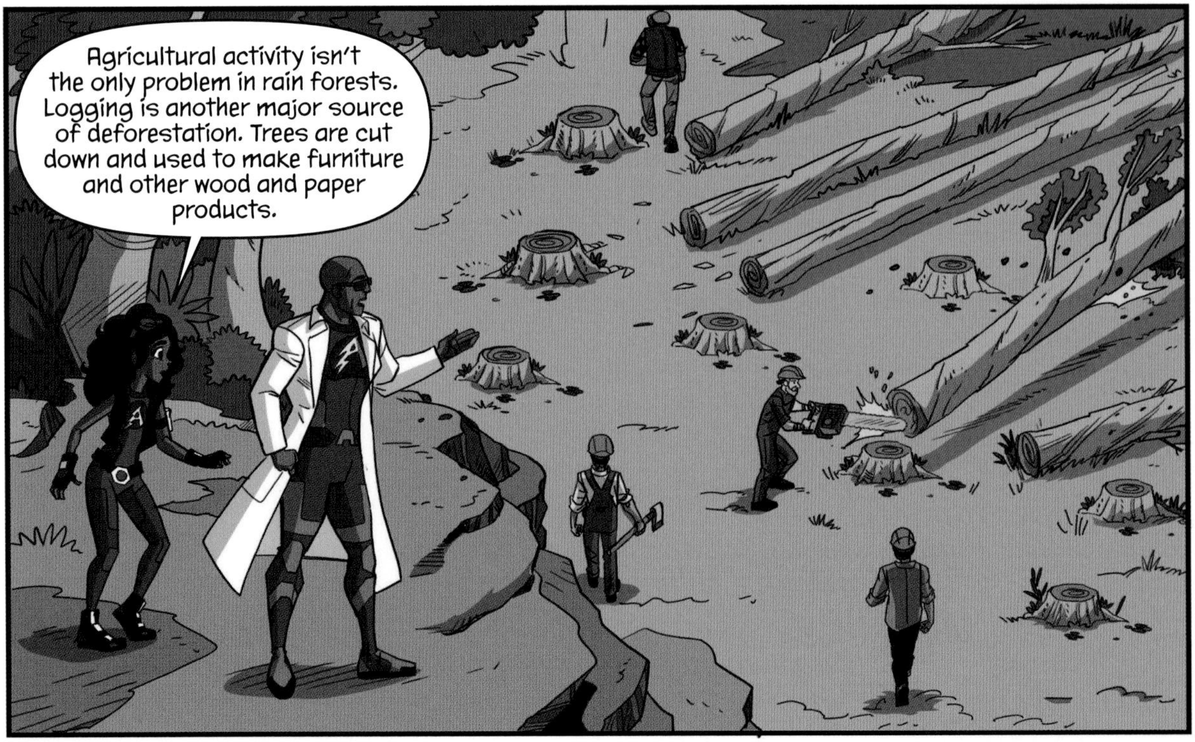
Agricultural activity isn't the only problem in rain forests. Logging is another major source of deforestation. Trees are cut down and used to make furniture and other wood and paper products.

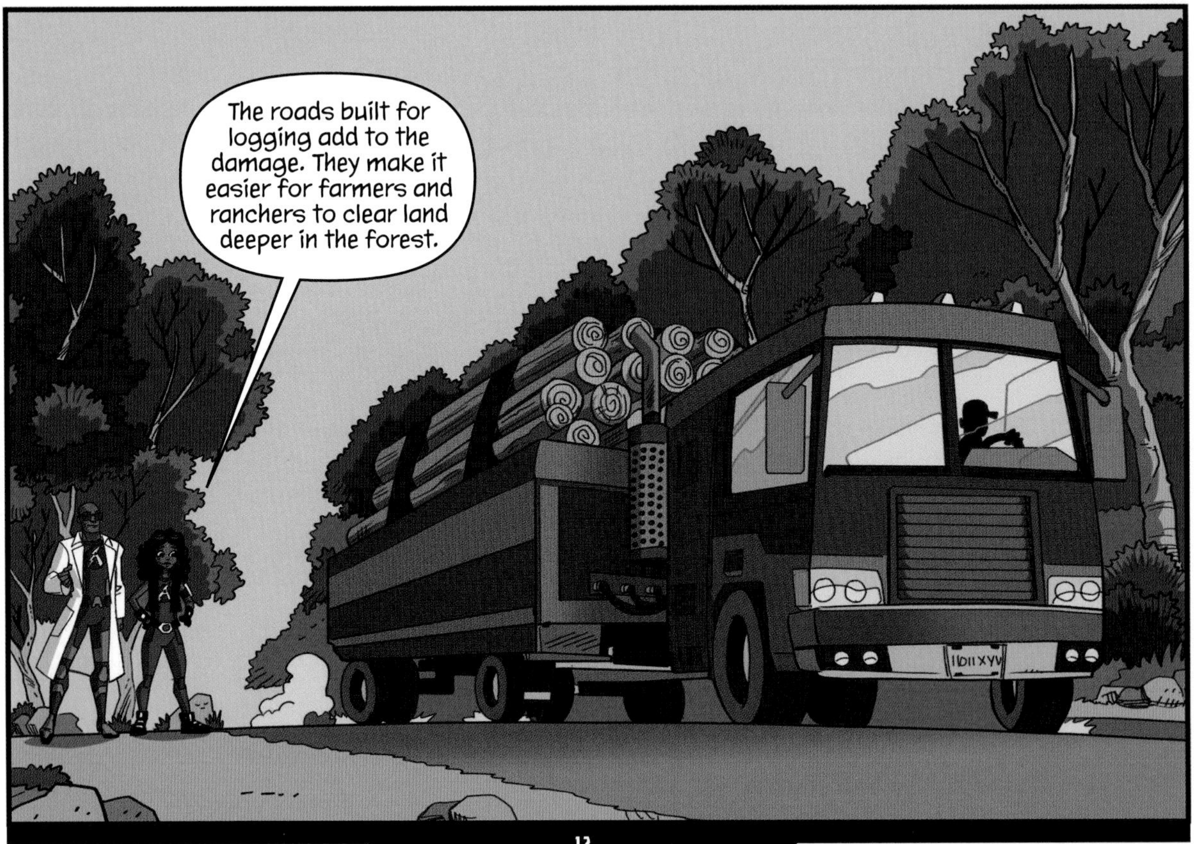
The roads built for logging add to the damage. They make it easier for farmers and ranchers to clear land deeper in the forest.
1011XYV

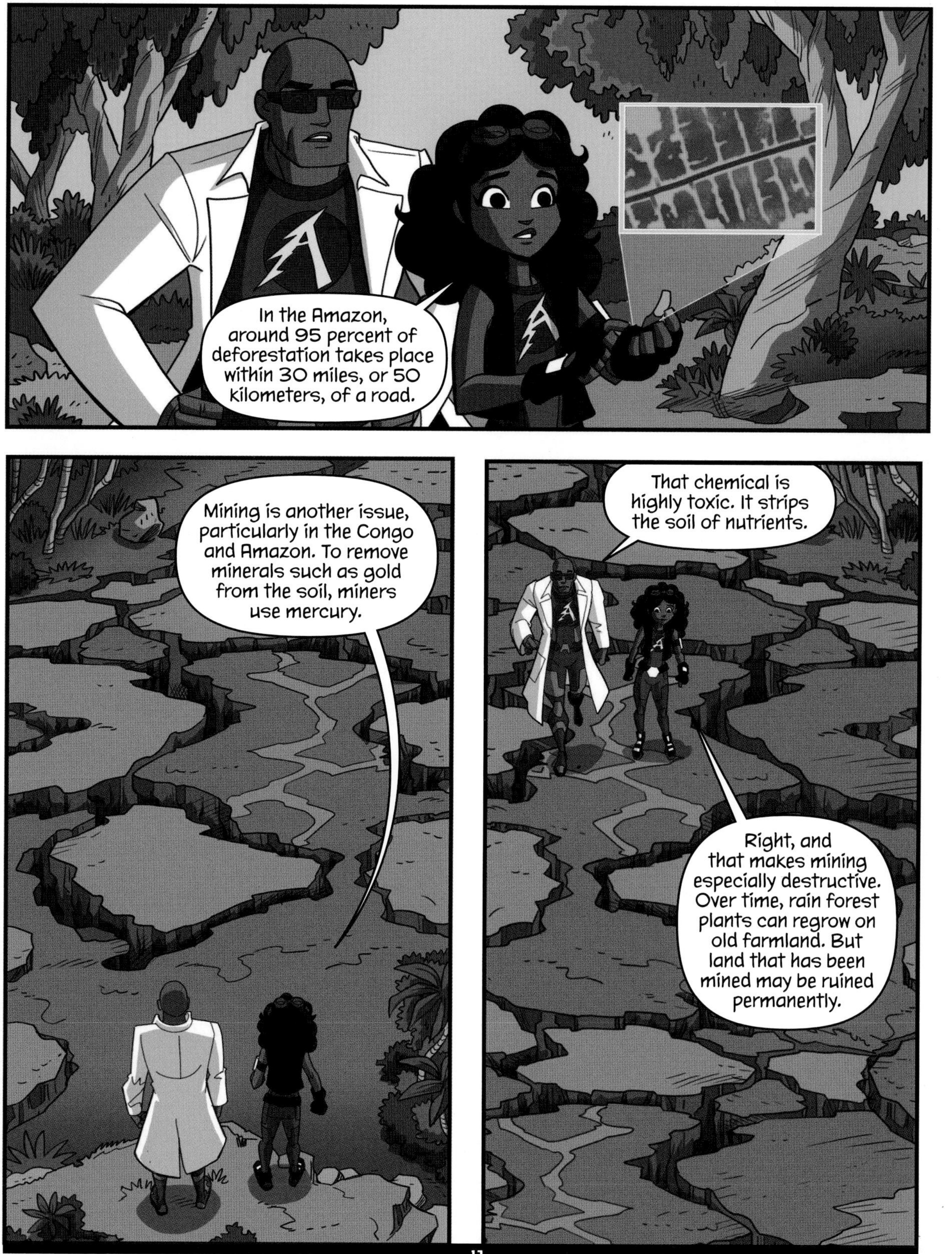
In the Amazon, around 95 percent of deforestation takes place within 30 miles, or 50 kilometers, of a road.
Mining is another issue, particularly in the Congo and Amazon. To remove minerals such as gold from the soil, miners use mercury.
That chemical is highly toxic. It strips the soil of nutrients.
Right, and that makes mining especially destructive. Over time, rain forest plants can regrow on old farmland. But land that has been mined may be ruined permanently.

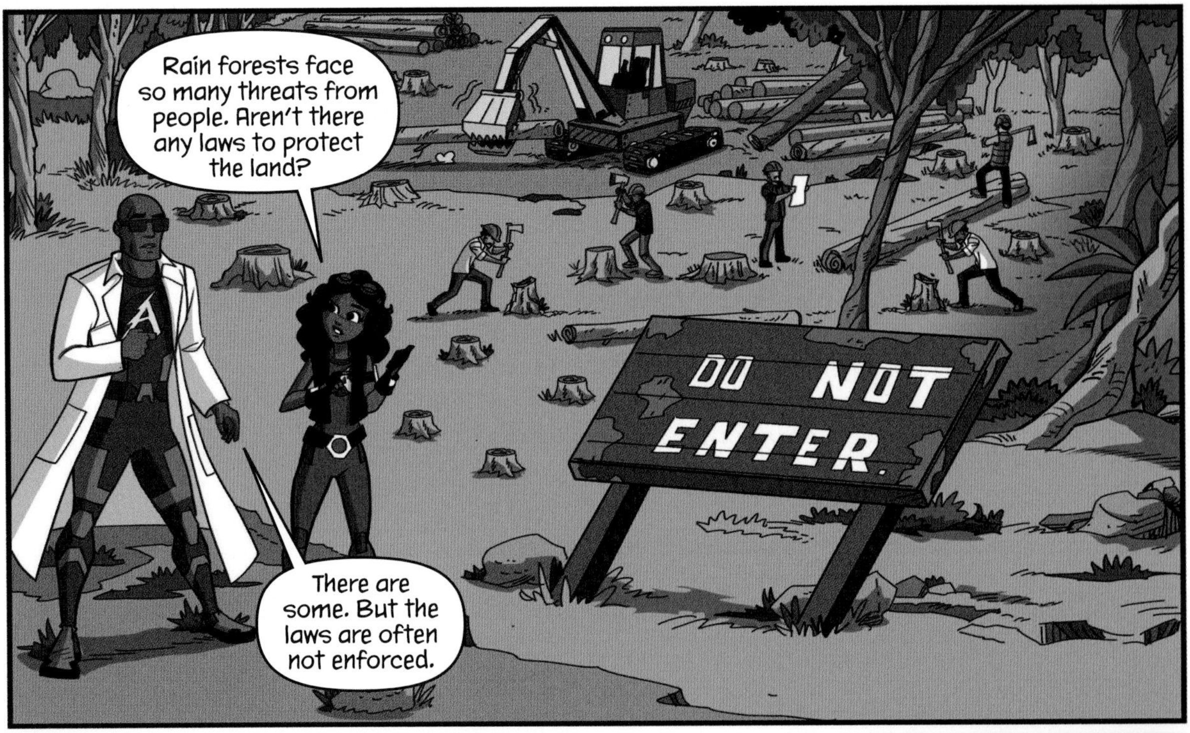
Rain forests face so many threats from people. Aren't there any laws to protect the land?
DO NOT ENTER.
There are some. But the laws are often not enforced.

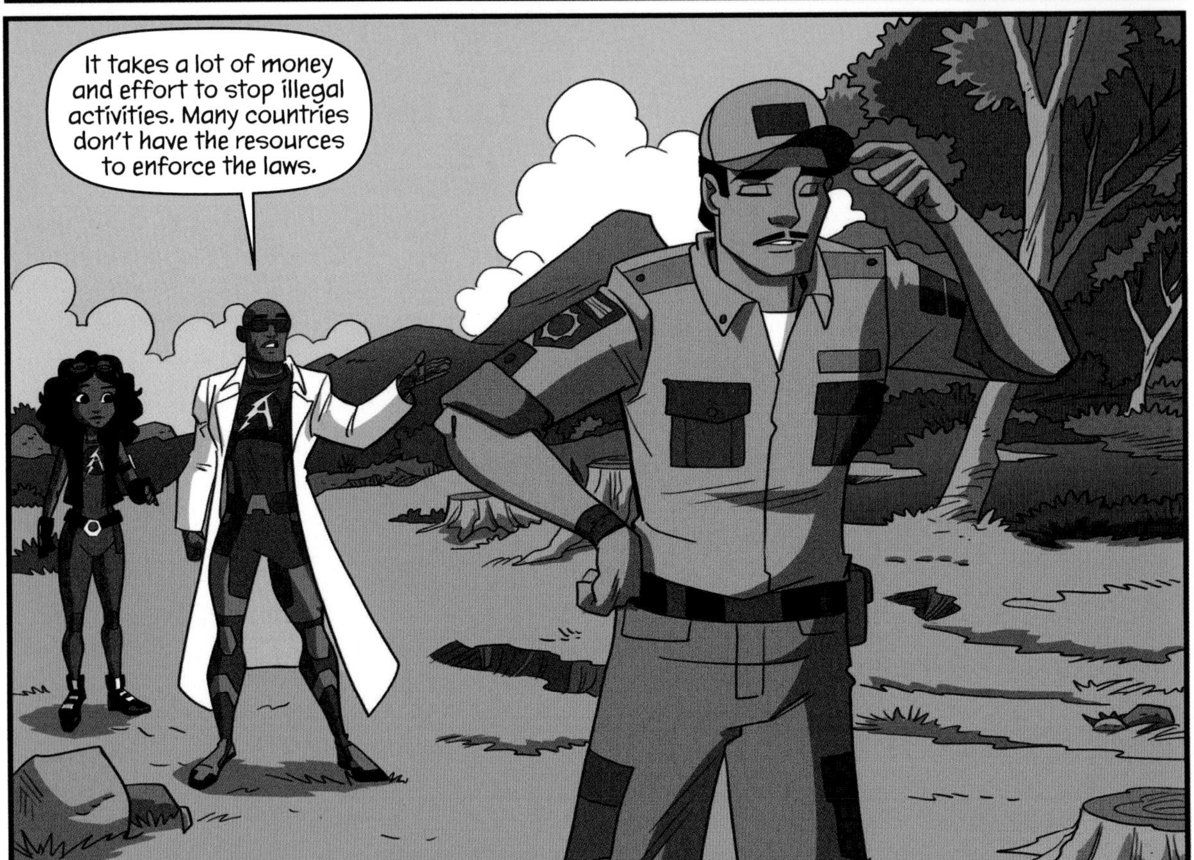
It takes a lot of money and effort to stop illegal activities. Many countries don't have the resources to enforce the laws.

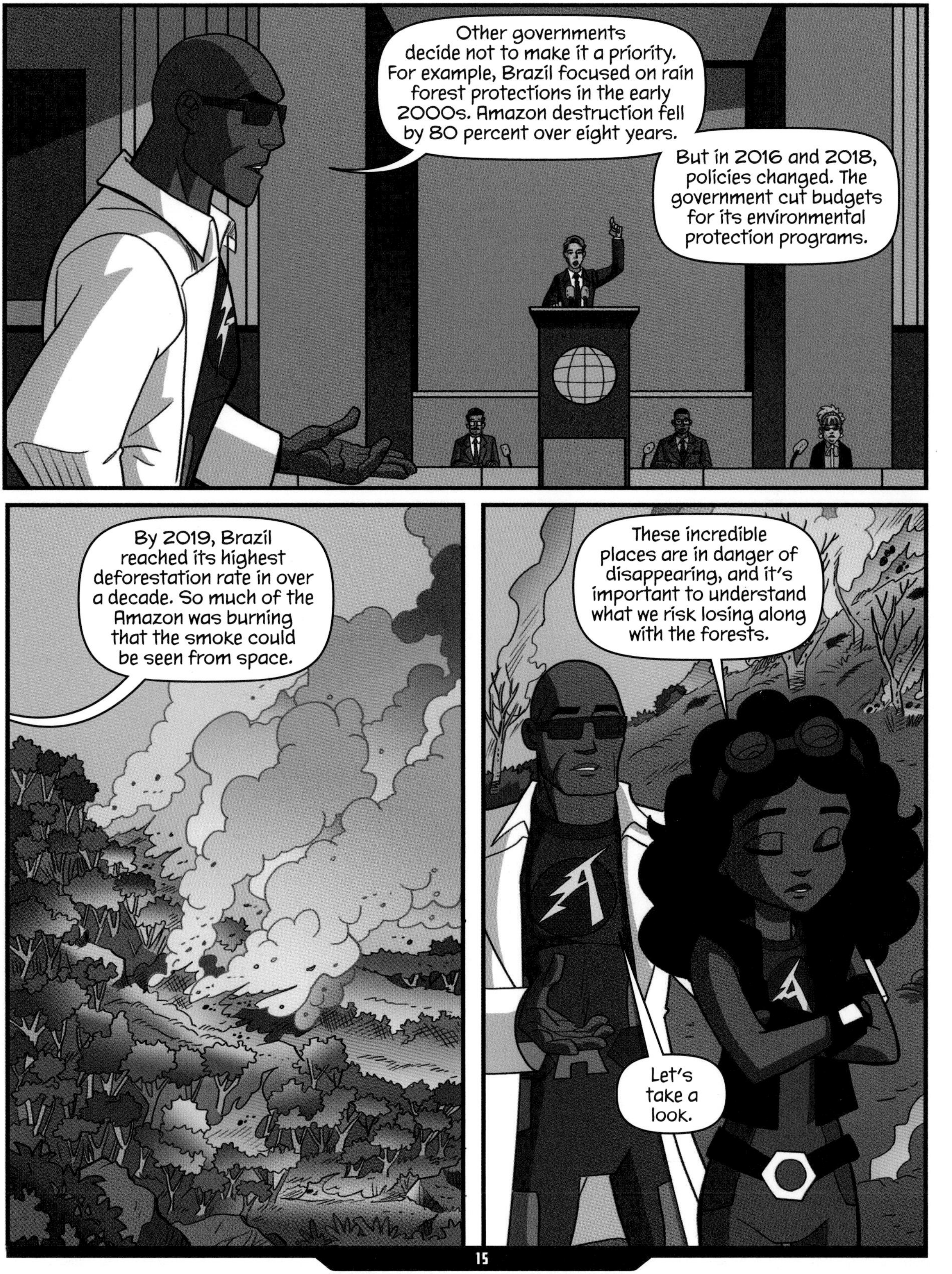
Other governments decide not to make it a priority. For example, Brazil focused on rain forest protections in the early 2000s. Amazon destruction fell by 80 percent over eight years.
But in 2016 and 2018, policies changed. The government cut budgets for its environmental protection programs.
By 2019, Brazil reached its highest deforestation rate in over a decade. So much of the Amazon was burning that the smoke could be seen from space.
These incredible places are in danger of disappearing, and it's important to understand what we risk losing along with the forests.
Let's take a look.

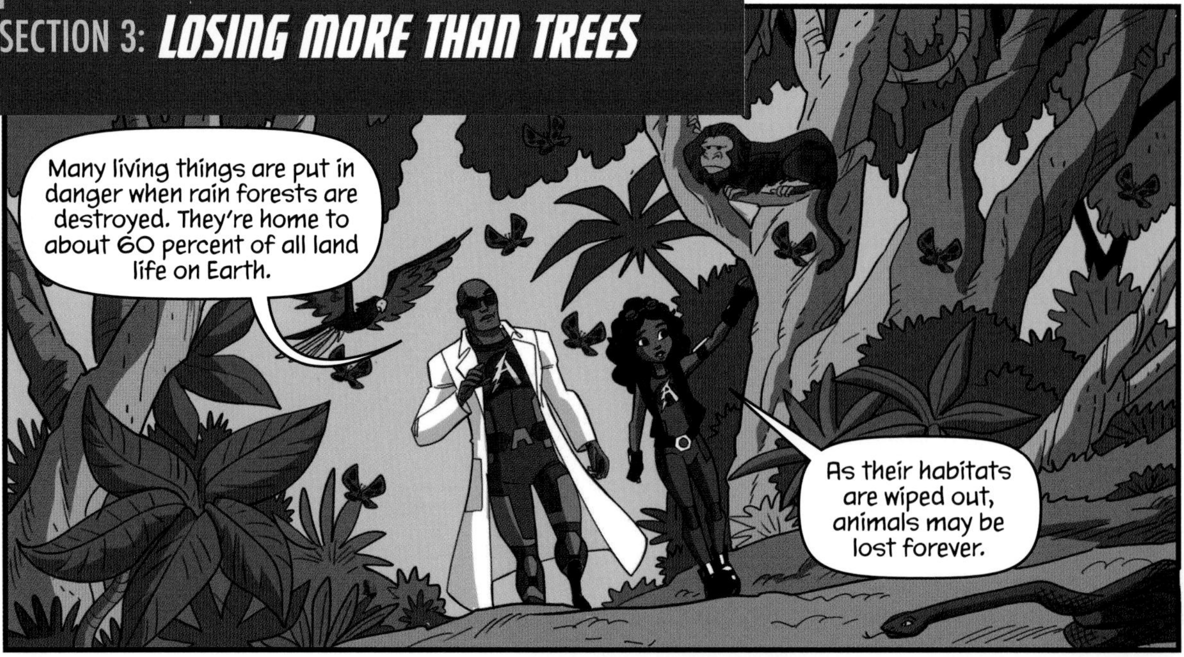
Many living things are put in danger when rain forests are destroyed. They're home to about 60 percent of all land life on Earth.
As their habitats are wiped out, animals may be lost forever.

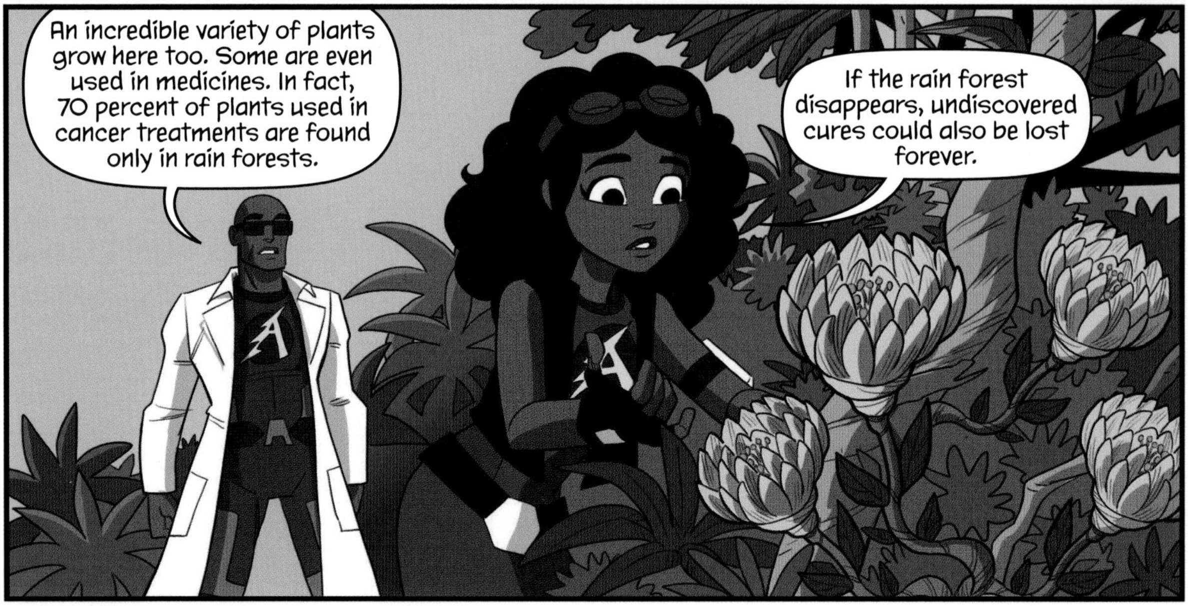
An incredible variety of plants grow here too. Some are even used in medicines. In fact, 70 percent of plants used in cancer treatments are found only in rain forests.
If the rain forest disappears, undiscovered cures could also be lost forever.

TOO MANY TO COUNT

Rain forests are home to an amazing variety of species. No one knows exactly how many. Estimates range from 3 to 50 million, and the numbers are still rising. For example, a two-year study by the World Wildlife Fund in the Amazon region discovered an average of one new species every two days. But with the high rate of tropical deforestation, scientists fear some species may become extinct before we even have a chance to discover them.

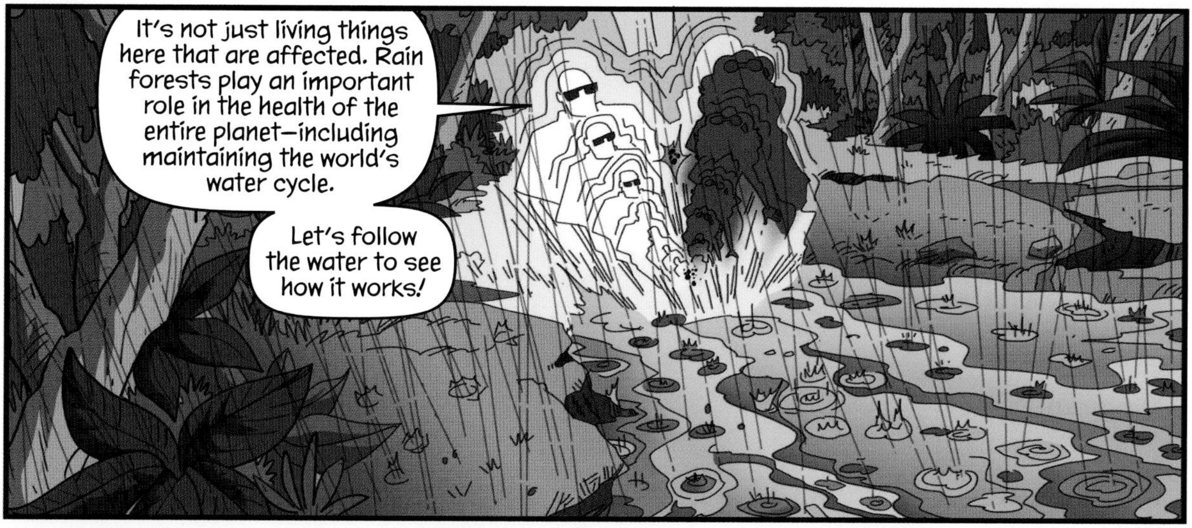
It's not just living things here that are affected. Rain forests play an important role in the health of the entire planet—including maintaining the world's water cycle.
Let's follow the water to see how it works!

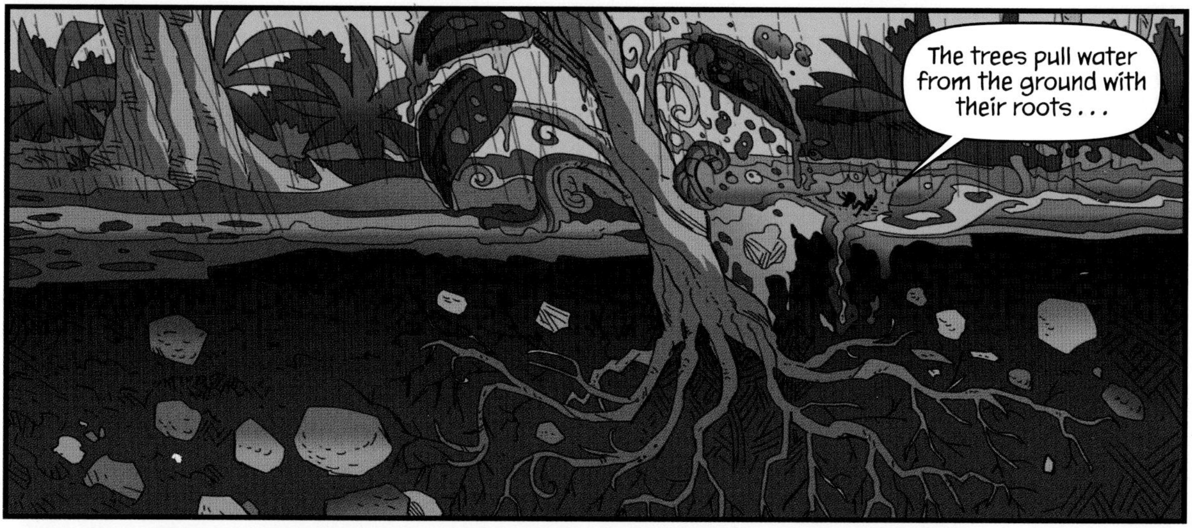
The trees pull water from the ground with their roots . . .

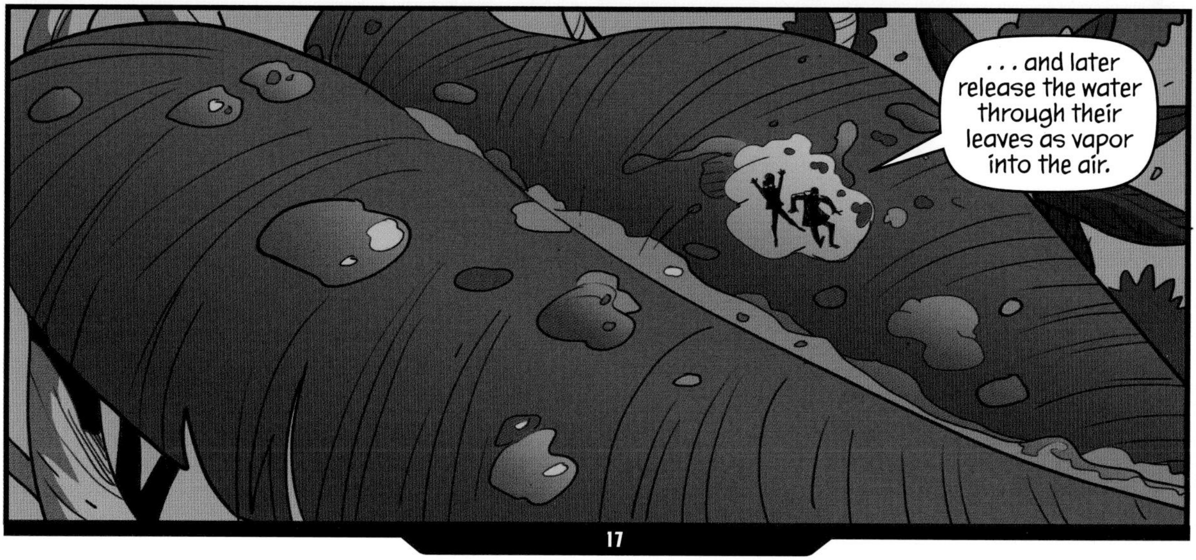
. . . and later release the water through their leaves as vapor into the air.

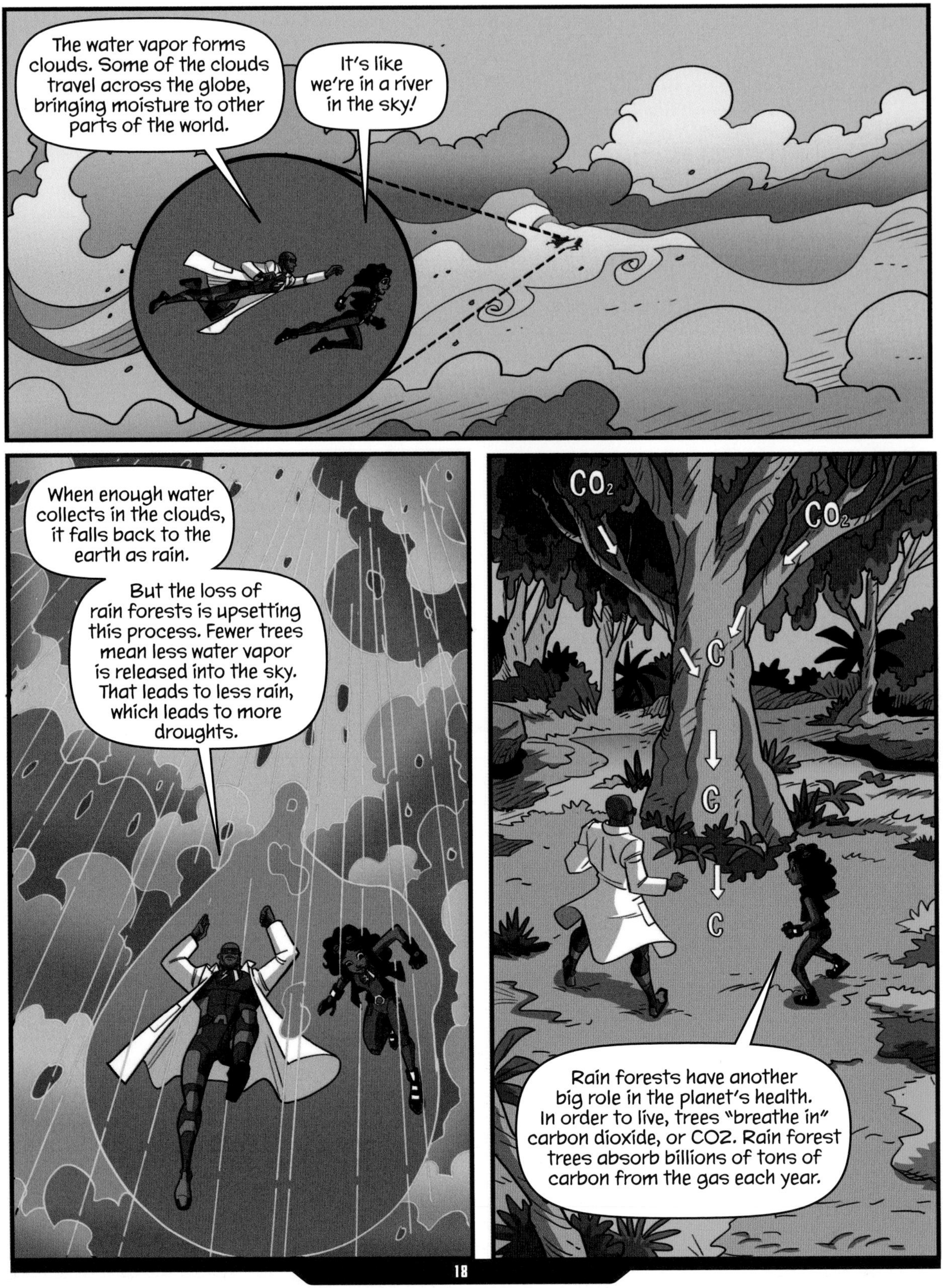
The water vapor forms clouds. Some of the clouds travel across the globe, bringing moisture to other parts of the world.
It's like we're in a river in the sky!
When enough water collects in the clouds, it falls back to the earth as rain.
But the loss of rain forests is upsetting this process. Fewer trees mean less water vapor is released into the sky. That leads to less rain, which leads to more droughts.
CO2
CO2
C
C
C
Rain forests have another big role in the planet's health. In order to live, trees "breathe in" carbon dioxide, or CO2. Rain forest trees absorb billions of tons of carbon from the gas each year.

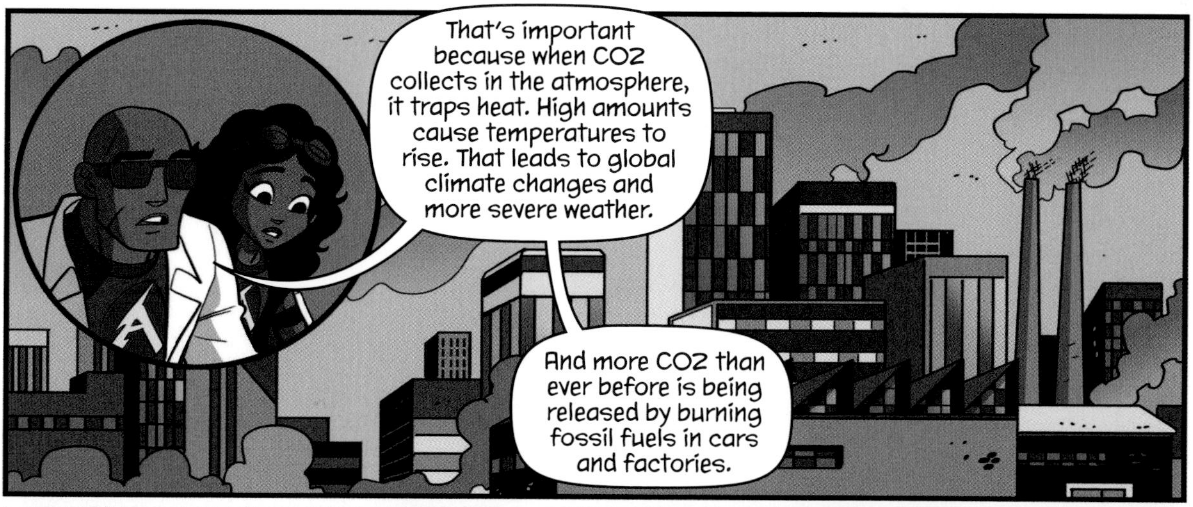
That's important because when CO2 collects in the atmosphere, it traps heat. High amounts cause temperatures to rise. That leads to global climate changes and more severe weather.
And more CO2 than ever before is being released by burning fossil fuels in cars and factories.

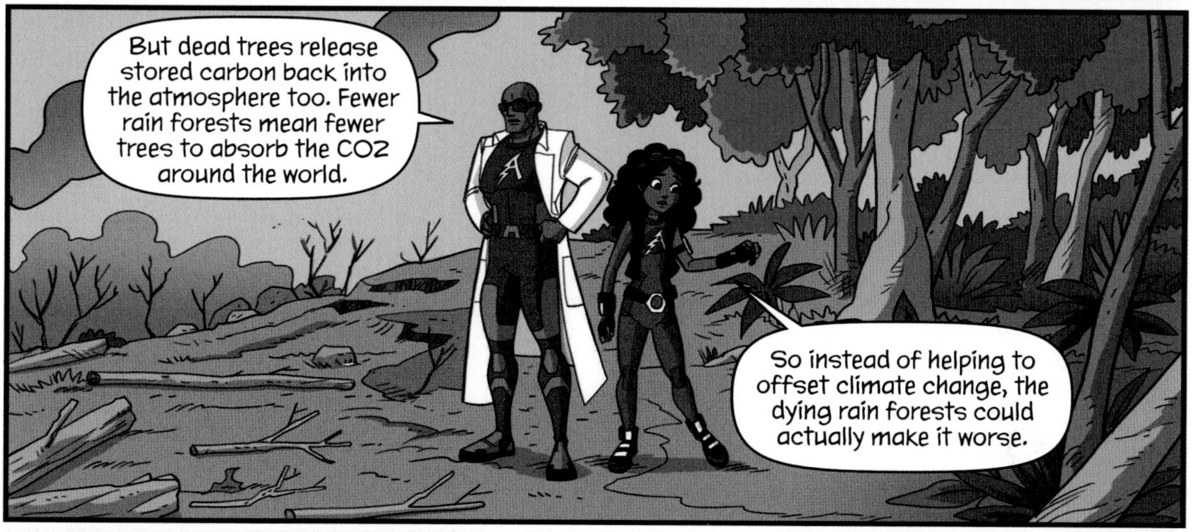
But dead trees release stored carbon back into the atmosphere too. Fewer rain forests mean fewer trees to absorb the CO2 around the world.
So instead of helping to offset climate change, the dying rain forests could actually make it worse.

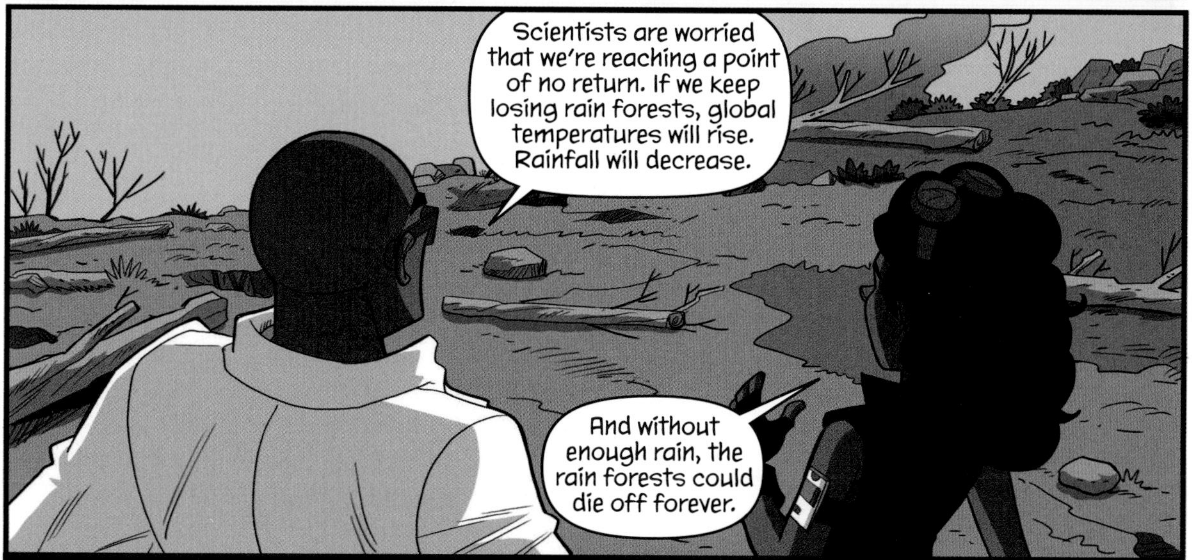
Scientists are worried that we're reaching a point of no return. If we keep losing rain forests, global temperatures will rise. Rainfall will decrease.
And without enough rain, the rain forests could die off forever.

SECTION 4: RESCUING THE RAIN FOREST

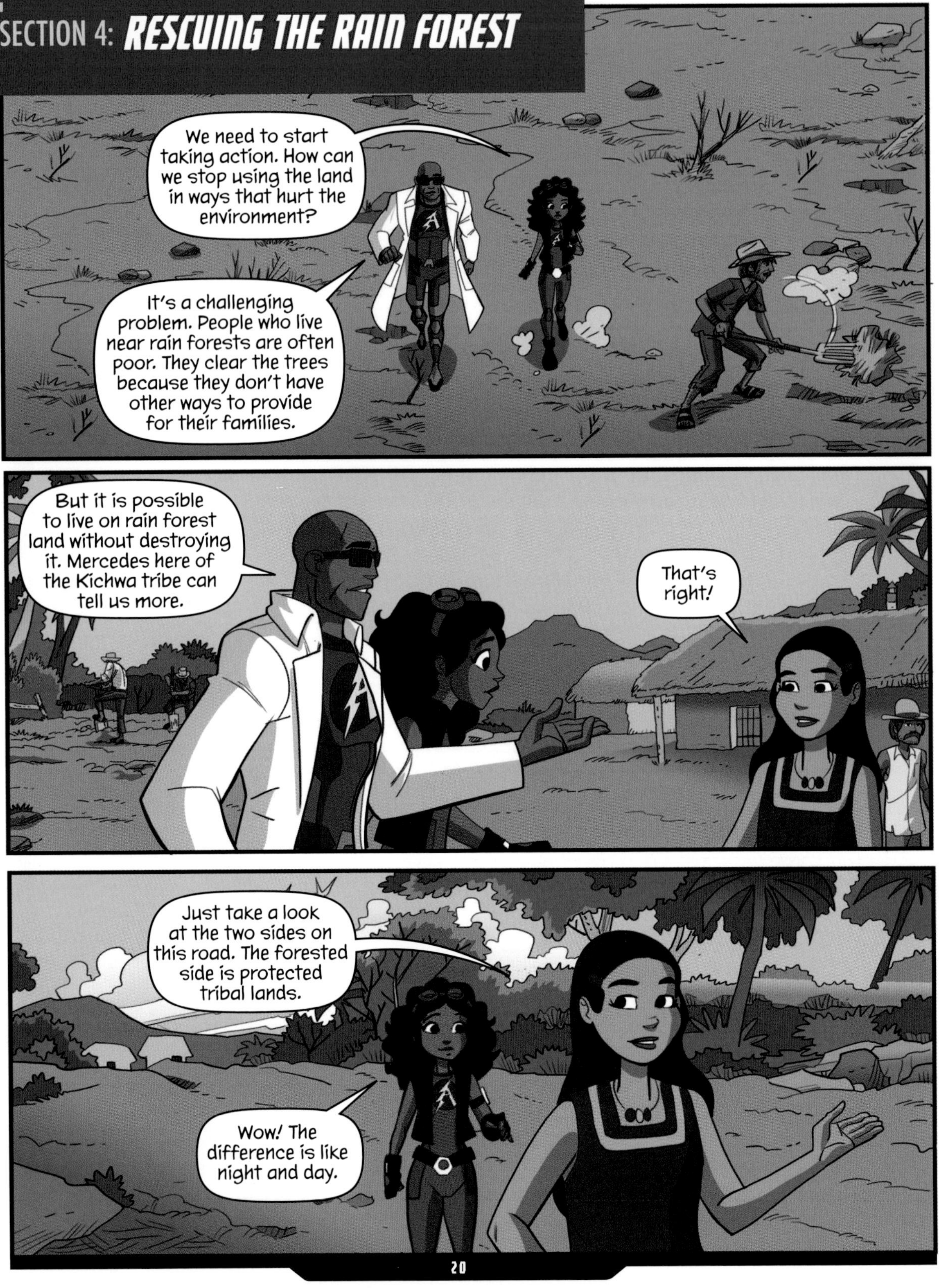
We need to start taking action. How can we stop using the land in ways that hurt the environment?
It's a challenging problem. People who live near rain forests are often poor. They clear the trees because they don't have other ways to provide for their families.
But it is possible to live on rain forest land without destroying it. Mercedes here of the Kichwa tribe can tell us more.
That's right!
Just take a look at the two sides on this road. The forested side is protected tribal lands.
Wow! The difference is like night and day.

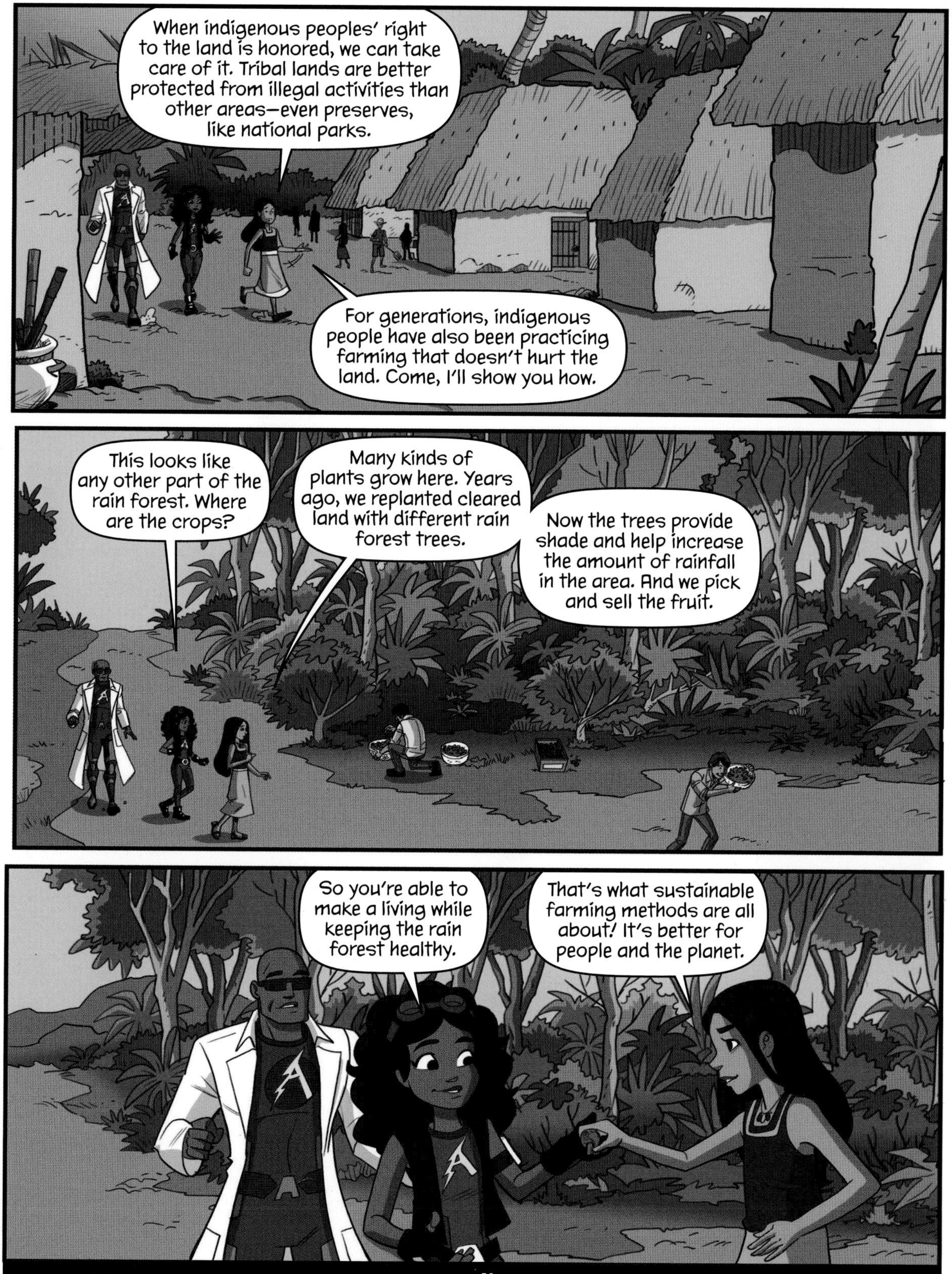
When indigenous peoples' right to the land is honored, we can take care of it. Tribal lands are better protected from illegal activities than other areas—even preserves, like national parks.
For generations, indigenous people have also been practicing farming that doesn't hurt the land. Come, I'll show you how.
This looks like any other part of the rain forest. Where are the crops?
Many kinds of plants grow here. Years ago, we replanted cleared land with different rain forest trees.
Now the trees provide shade and help increase the amount of rainfall in the area. And we pick and sell the fruit.
So you're able to make a living while keeping the rain forest healthy.
That's what sustainable farming methods are all about! It's better for people and the planet.

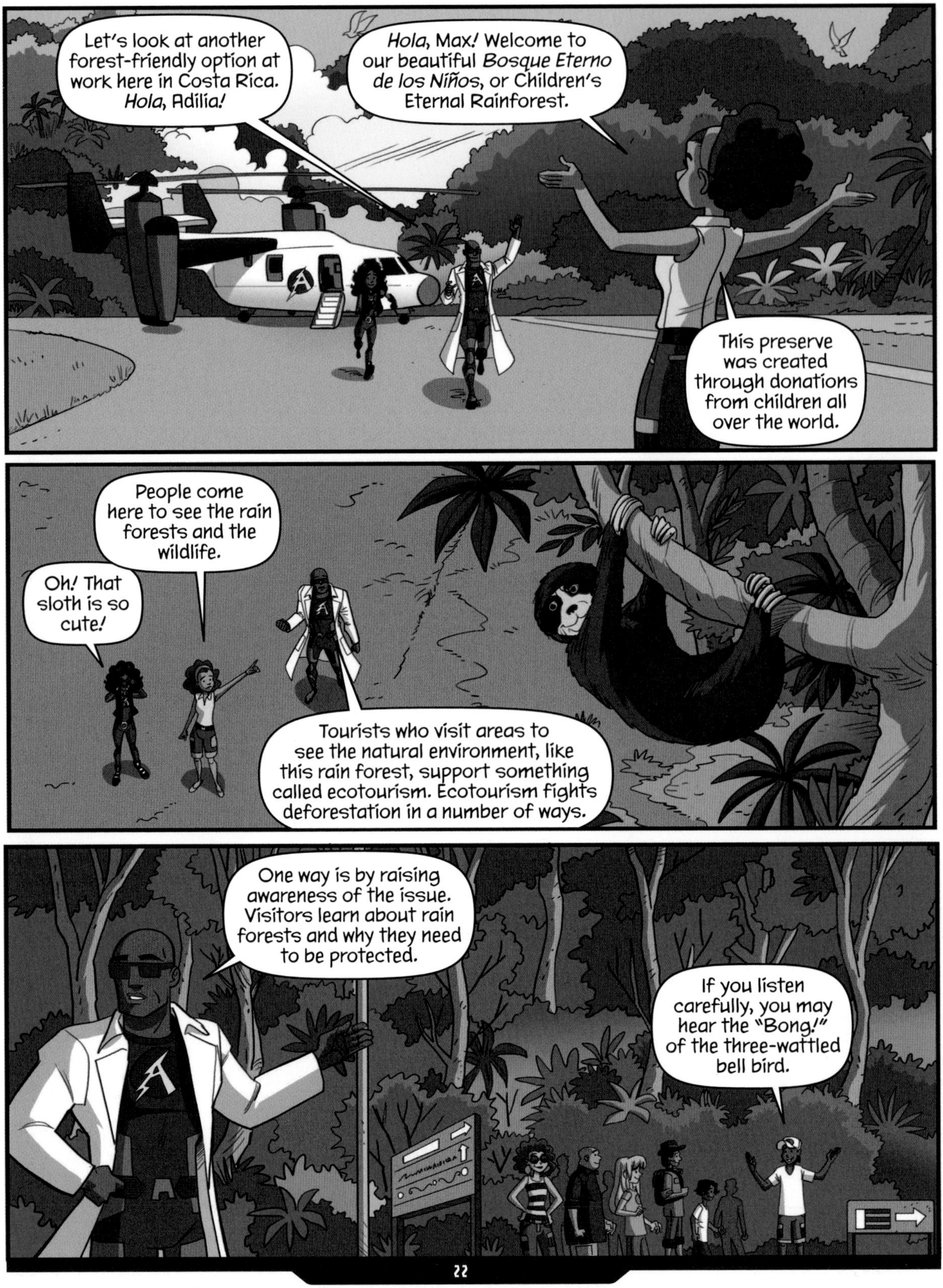

Let's look at another forest-friendly option at work here in Costa Rica. *Hola*, Adilia!
Hola, Max! Welcome to our beautiful *Bosque Eterno de los Niños*, or Children's Eternal Rainforest.
This preserve was created through donations from children all over the world.
People come here to see the rain forests and the wildlife.
Oh! That sloth is so cute!
Tourists who visit areas to see the natural environment, like this rain forest, support something called ecotourism. Ecotourism fights deforestation in a number of ways.
One way is by raising awareness of the issue. Visitors learn about rain forests and why they need to be protected.
If you listen carefully, you may hear the "Bong!" of the three-wattled bell bird.

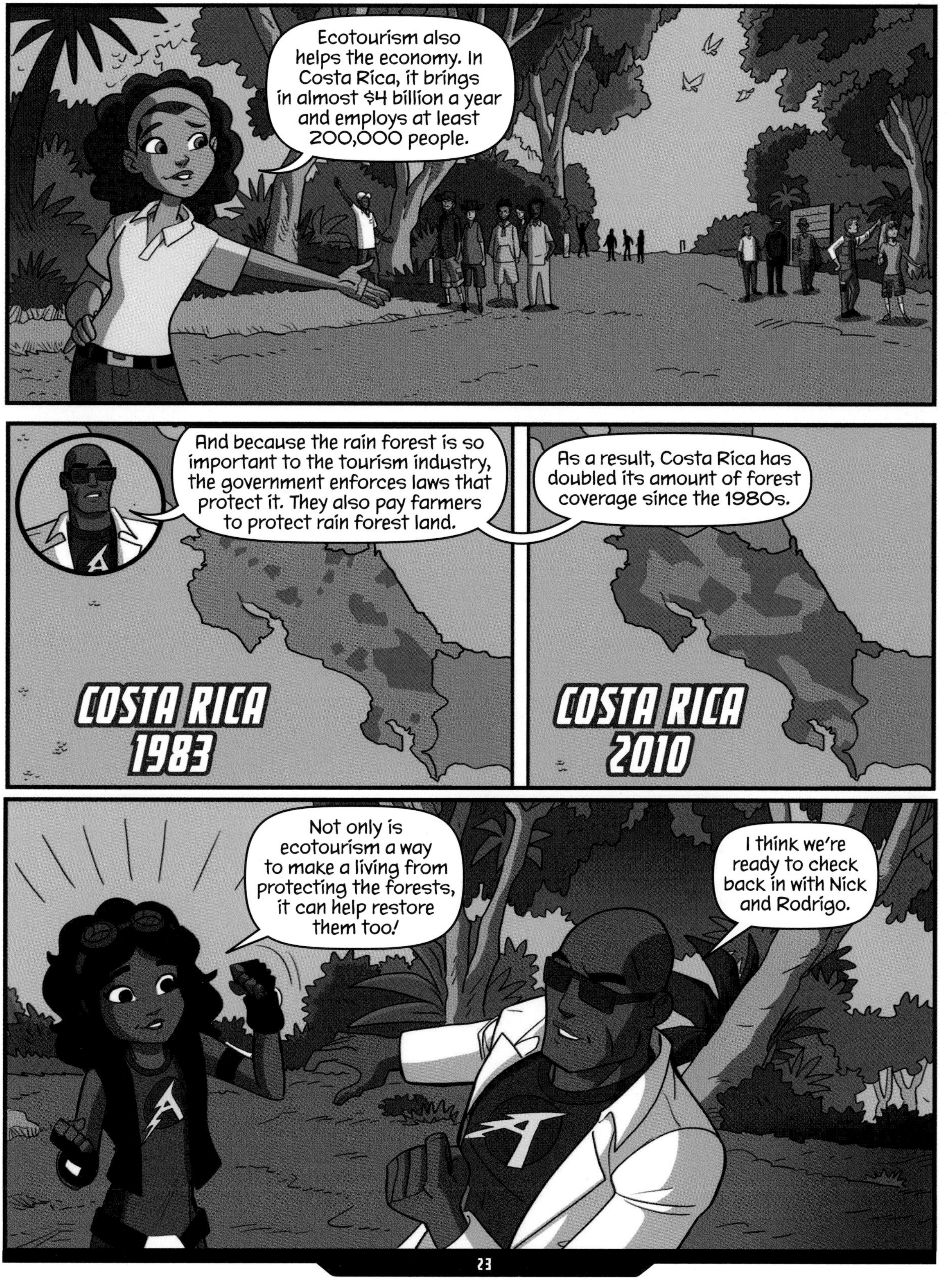

Ecotourism also helps the economy. In Costa Rica, it brings in almost $4 billion a year and employs at least 200,000 people.
And because the rain forest is so important to the tourism industry, the government enforces laws that protect it. They also pay farmers to protect rain forest land.
As a result, Costa Rica has doubled its amount of forest coverage since the 1980s.
COSTA RICA 1983
COSTA RICA 2010
Not only is ecotourism a way to make a living from protecting the forests, it can help restore them too!
I think we're ready to check back in with Nick and Rodrigo.

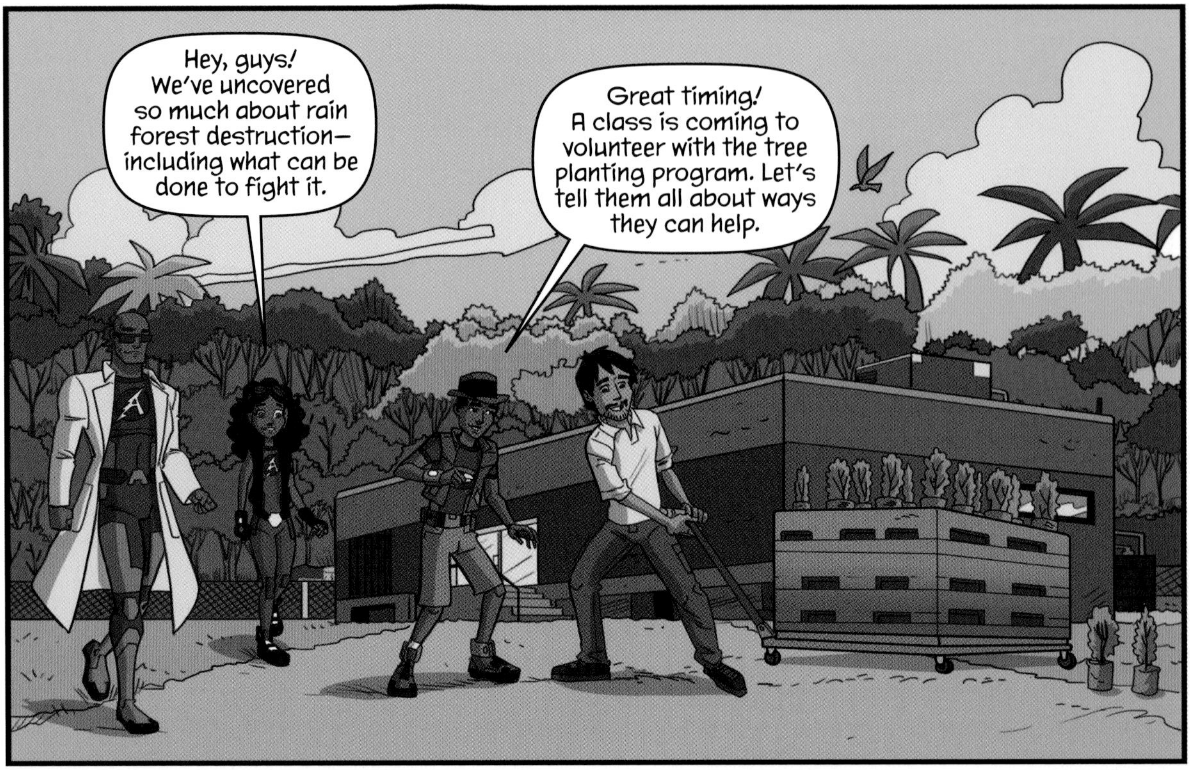
Hey, guys! We've uncovered so much about rain forest destruction—including what can be done to fight it.
Great timing! A class is coming to volunteer with the tree planting program. Let's tell them all about ways they can help.

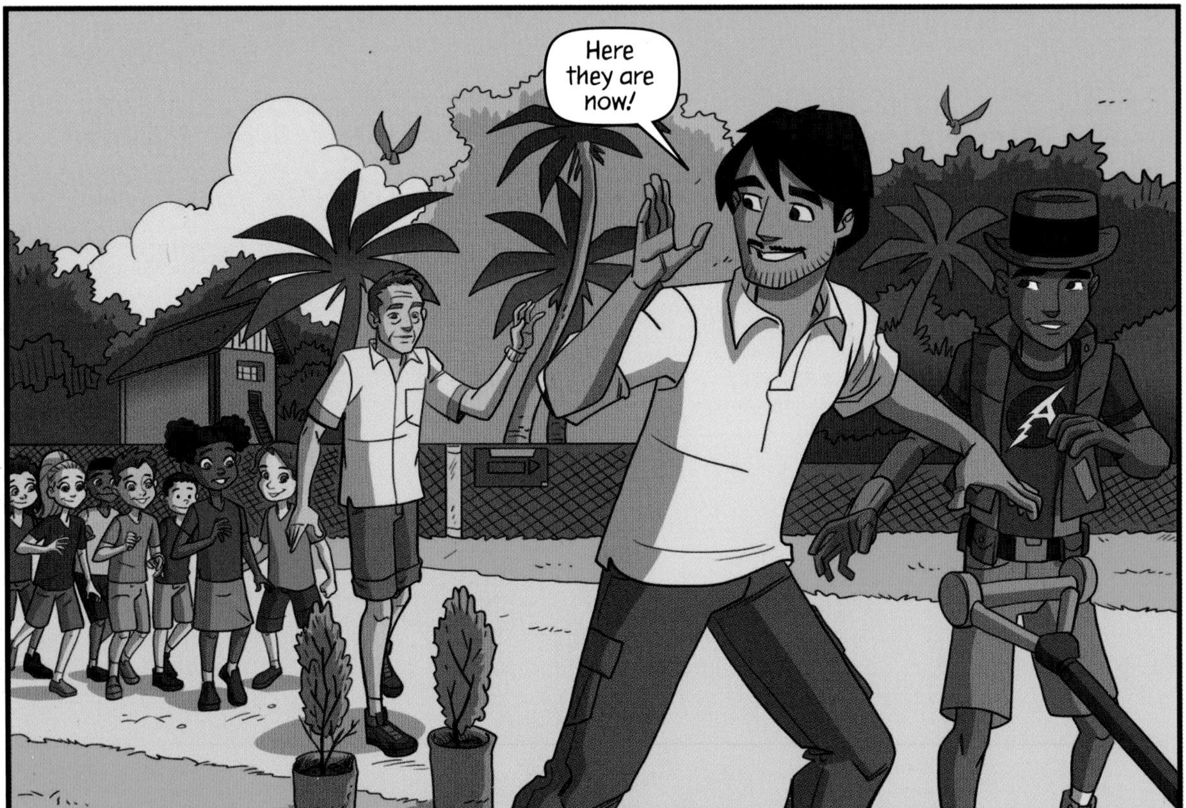
Here they are now!

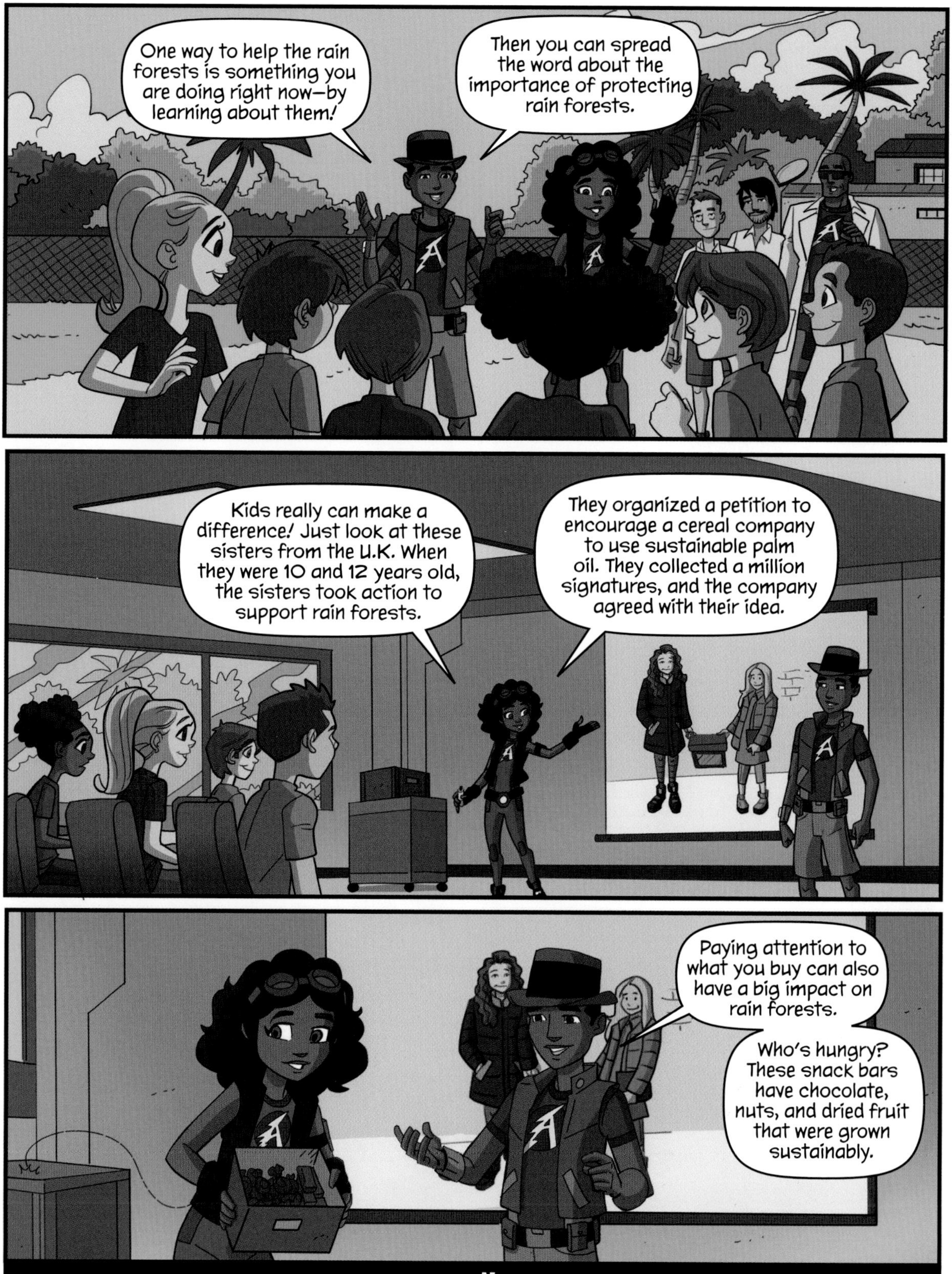
One way to help the rain forests is something you are doing right now—by learning about them!
Then you can spread the word about the importance of protecting rain forests.
Kids really can make a difference! Just look at these sisters from the U.K. When they were 10 and 12 years old, the sisters took action to support rain forests.
They organized a petition to encourage a cereal company to use sustainable palm oil. They collected a million signatures, and the company agreed with their idea.
Paying attention to what you buy can also have a big impact on rain forests.
Who's hungry? These snack bars have chocolate, nuts, and dried fruit that were grown sustainably.

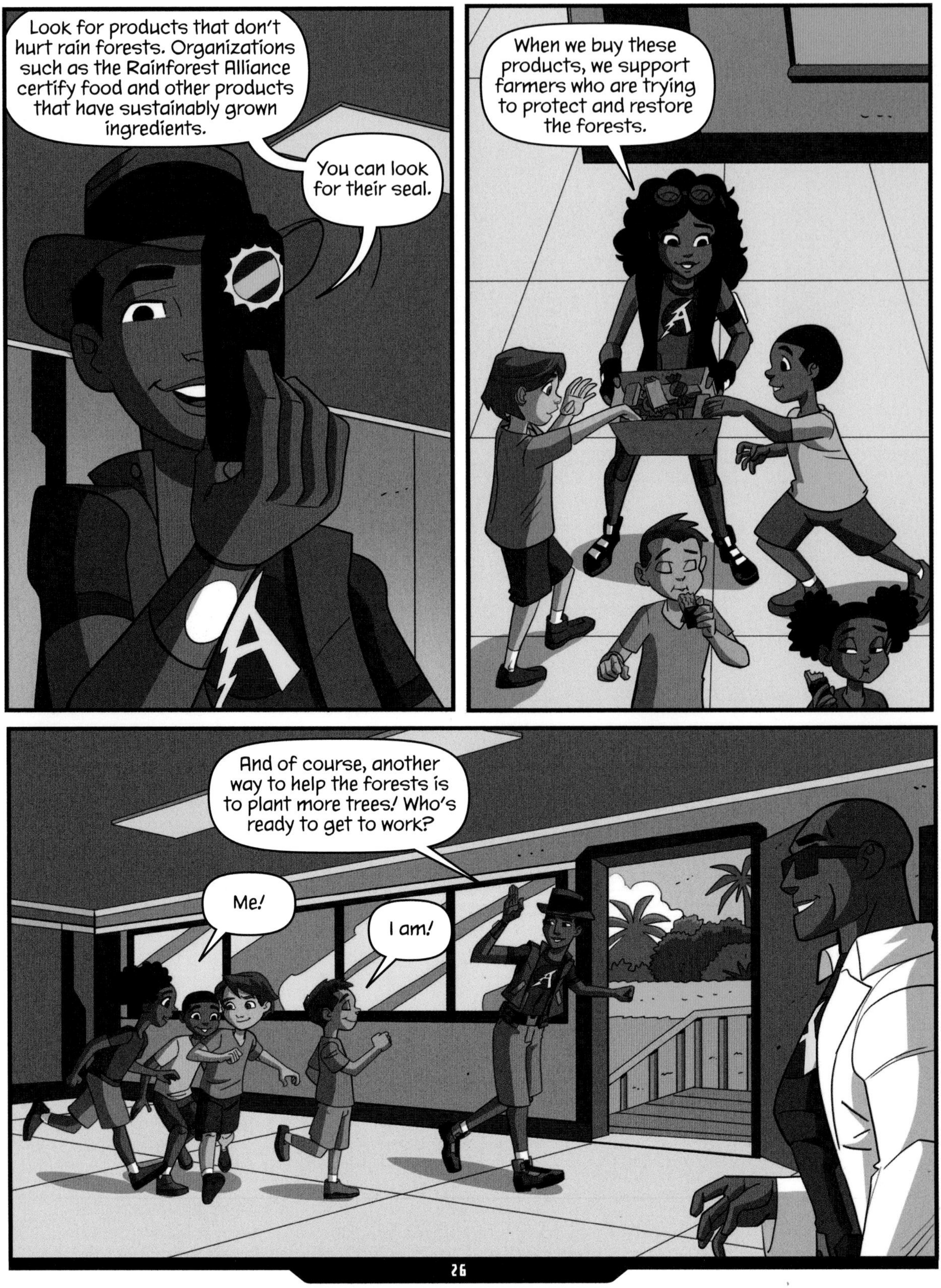
Look for products that don't hurt rain forests. Organizations such as the Rainforest Alliance certify food and other products that have sustainably grown ingredients.
You can look for their seal.
When we buy these products, we support farmers who are trying to protect and restore the forests.
And of course, another way to help the forests is to plant more trees! Who's ready to get to work?
Me!
I am!

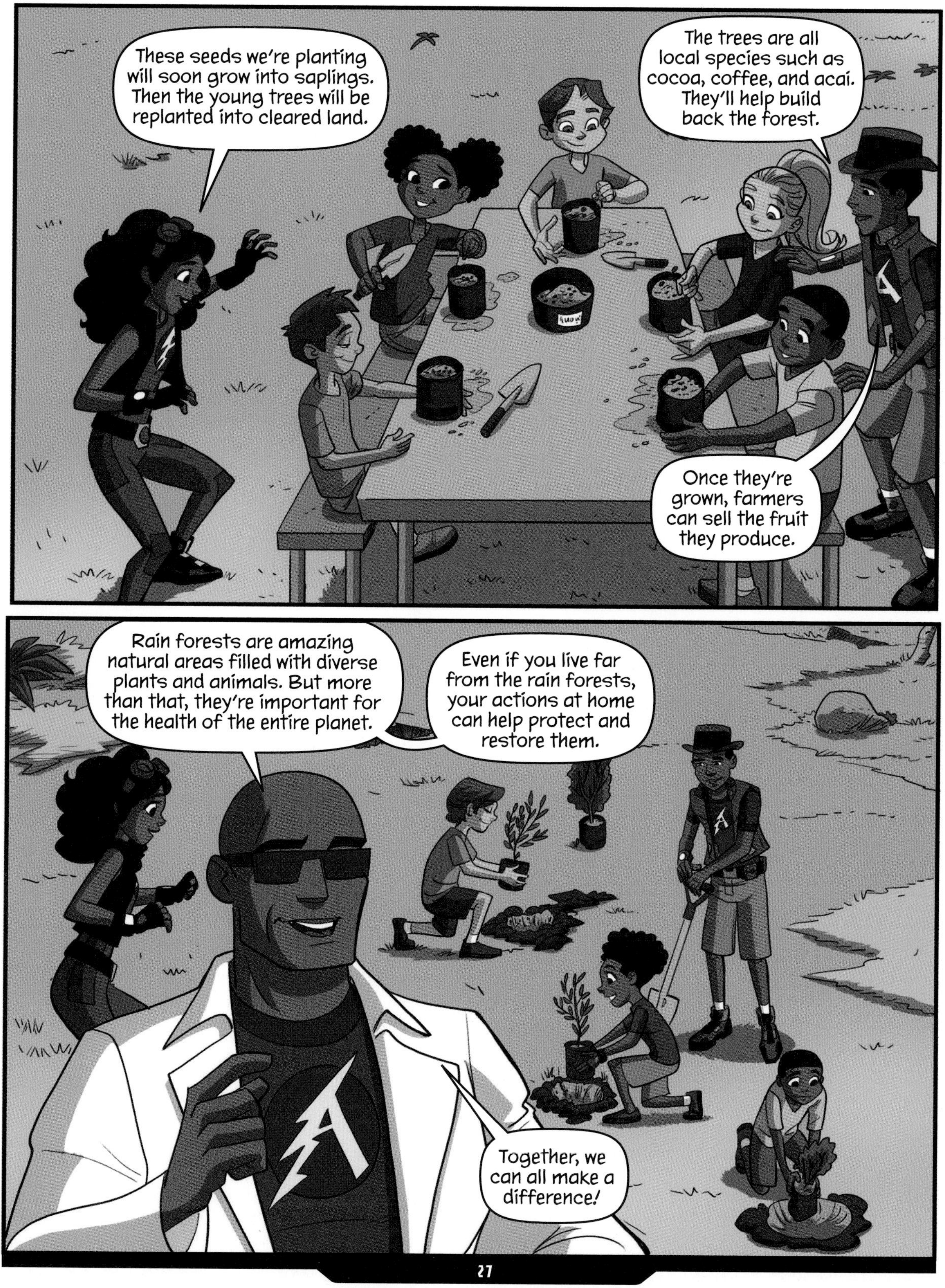
These seeds we're planting will soon grow into saplings. Then the young trees will be replanted into cleared land.
The trees are all local species such as cocoa, coffee, and acai. They'll help build back the forest.
Once they're grown, farmers can sell the fruit they produce.
Rain forests are amazing natural areas filled with diverse plants and animals. But more than that, they're important for the health of the entire planet.
Even if you live far from the rain forests, your actions at home can help protect and restore them.
Together, we can all make a difference!

HOW KIDS SAVED A RAIN FOREST

The issue of rain forest destruction can sometimes feel too big and too far away to do anything about it. But one group of children believed they should try.

During the 1980s, rain forests were experiencing some of the highest rates of deforestation in history. In 1987, far from the tropics, a group of 9- and 10-year-old schoolchildren in Sweden learned about rain forests. They watched videos of trees being cut down and burned. Upset, the children asked what they could do to help. Finally, one student asked, "Why can't we buy some rain forest?"

It seemed like a far-fetched solution—but it was one that could protect some rain forest land. The children were determined to try. The class started holding bake sales and performing plays to raise money. They were delighted to learn the $240 they raised could be used to purchase a dozen acres of rain forest for protection in Costa Rica.

Inspired by their success, the class kept working to raise money. A television station broadcast a performance by the class to raise awareness about the rain forests. More money was raised, and more children got involved. The Swedish government gave an $80,000 grant toward the purchase of more rain forest. By the end of the year, the children had raised $100,000. But they were just getting started. Word kept spreading, and by 1992, children from 44 countries helped raise $2 million.